CRACCO
IN GALLERIA

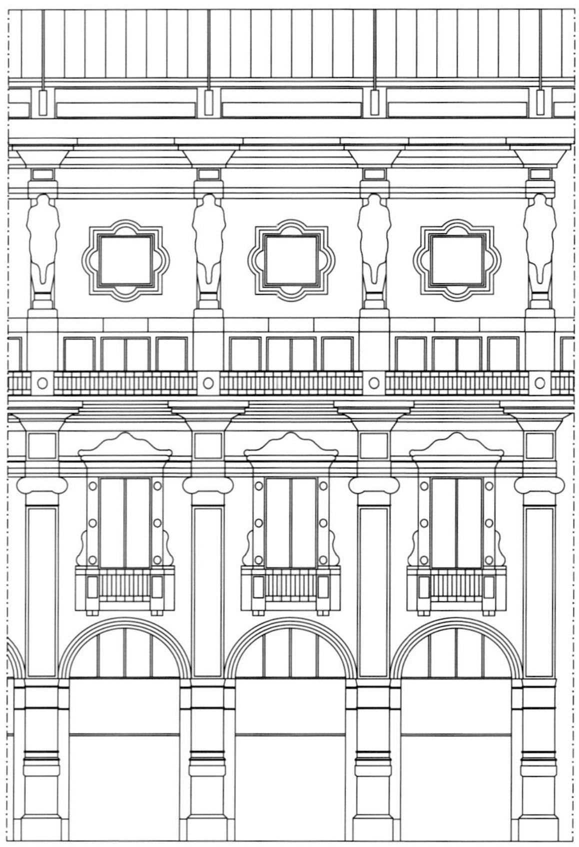

CRACCO IN GALLERIA

DREAMED OF BY

CARLO CRACCO

LUCA SACCHI

IMAGINED BY

MAURIZIO CATTELAN

PIERPAOLO FERRARI

ALBERTO ZANETTI

SEBASTIANO MASTROENI

WRITTEN BY

GABRIELE ZANATTA

Φ

THE GALLERIA: MILAN'S 'SALON'

The Galleria di Milano – designed and built in 1861, the year that the kingdom of Italy was born – bears the name of the first king, Victor Emmanuel II. Above all, it is the product of all those distinctive personalities who conceived, designed, painted and sang in it, as well as those who simply frequented it. The story began with Antonio Beretta, a progressive mayor of Milan, who wanted to tear down the old houses between the neoclassical Teatro alla Scala (designed by Giuseppe Piermarini in 1778) and the late Gothic Duomo. In 1860, Beretta called for a public tender to completely redesign the residential area linking these two symbolic masterpieces of the city. After the first tender, other two followed (in 1861 and 1863) and, in the end, the chosen design was by Giuseppe Mengoni, an architect and engineer of Romagnan origins and extraordinary moral virtues.

Giuseppe Mengoni was a family man who led a sober and serious life, always acting as an honest and impeccable professional. Amid this somewhat subdued conduct, however, he still found time for festivities, setting up firework displays, lights, flares and decorations for a whole variety of celebrations.

The 100,000 people who walk every day through the Galleria with noses turned up are indebted to this visionary gentleman, with his enthusiasm for wrought-iron architecture, a style that was not only foreshadowed by the distinctive early nineteenth-century 'covered passages' of Paris but eventually culminated in the Eiffel Tower itself. For the Galleria, Mengoni designed and built a gallery on a cruciform plan, underneath a 93,000-square-metre (1,001,044-square-foot) wrought-iron and meshed-glass roof. This neo-Renaissance roof, imposing and luminous, soared above a 'labyrinth of 1,260 rooms including halls, corridors, staircases, passages, ravines, vestibules, tunnels, cellars, courtyards and patios', as the journalist and writer Dino Buzzati described it, in the 1960s. In the two and a half years between the laying of the Galleria's foundation stone by King Victor Emmanuel (7 March 1865) and its public inauguration (15 September 1867), it was already clear that this great post-unification work – conceived to pay homage to the bourgeois taste of the time – would become a popular meeting place: the veritable Salotto di Milano ('salon of Milan') as the modern inhabitants of the city have dubbed it. Architects, writers, painters, shopkeepers, poets and restaurateurs: the Galleria has always been a free-access theatre in which both actors and spectators could have their say. Open to all, its sumptuous furnishings are available to everyone. The Galleria is the place par excellence that best expresses the city's dedication to hospitality, cultural integration and cosmopolitanism. As the immortal phrase goes: 'One is not born Milanese but becomes it.' The Galleria is Milan's iron and glass haven that for decades has welcomed everyone. Even at night, with its street lamps, first gas and then electric, it provides illumination of all kinds for those who come with good intentions.

In the first decade of the twentieth century, the Galleria was the setting for the corrosive expressiveness of the writings and plays of Filippo Tommaso Marinetti, the founder of the Italian Futurist movement, one of the earliest and most important artistic avant-garde movements in Europe. It was also here that the *Corriere della Sera*, now the most widely read daily newspaper in the country, was not only established but immediately enriched by the colourful tales of the journalist Luigi Capuana, set in 'the indispensable and vital centre, the heart of the city'.

According to another journalist, Giuseppe Marotta, 'The Galleria is home and office, street and umbrella, it is everything for me with its restaurants, cafés, billiard-halls, pharmacies, baths, hairdressers, shoe-shiners, busy men, and shapely, elegant women, as well as shade in the summer and infrared rays in the winter. In a hundred ways, the gallery nourishes us'. And it also resurrects us – there were even workshops for the embalming of animals in the Galleria.

It was under the *ca' de veder* ('house of glass' in the Milanese dialect) that the first 'creative agencies' of the post-war period began to spring up, gradually establishing the city's graphic design supremacy.

Milan was at once transformed into a kind of sounding board, vibrating and amplifying the notes of the Teatro alla Scala, located at the end of one of the four arms of Mengoni's cruciform plan, as musicians and librettists of such calibre as Giacomo Puccini or Arrigo Boito shuttled between cafés, enjoying their quiet *struscio* ('stroll'). The Galleria was the 'think tank' in which Umberto Boccioni, another prominent Futurist, translated his provocations into paintings, such as the famous *Rissa in Galleria*, portraying a mob swarming in front of Gaspare Campari's bar as they strove to separate two quarrelling prostitutes.

'Whenever a great piece of political news spreads like wildfire through the city, or a huge anniversary is commemorated, we see an endless stream of people coursing through the streets, day and night... and this vast human family chatters, glimmers and smoulders under the glare of a thousand little flames like jewelled crowns' (Emilio De Marchi, *Milano e i suoi dintorni*, 1881).

The Galleria in a postcard from the early 1900s

The Galleria was the workshop in which Milan's fashion district took shape: it was under the central 'Ottagono' that Mario Prada, Miuccia's grandfather, opened a shop in 1913, where he began selling bags, trunks and leather goods. It was here that Guglielmo Miani, a prodigious tailor of Apulian birth, designed clothes for Buster Keaton, Charlie Chaplin and Fausto Coppi. And all this was going on at the same time as the voices of the modernist poet Giuseppe Ungaretti and two Nobel Prize winners for literature, Eugenio Montale and Salvatore Quasimodo, were heard in its streets. A true barometer of city life, the Galleria has also staged tragedies great and small, including the accident (or perhaps even the suicide) that befell its own architect, Giuseppe Mengoni, when he fell from the scaffolding before his work was finished, 'making a deathbed of his own finished work', as the king said in his eulogy. The Galleria was also the place in which

'Afterward when I could get around on crutches we went to dinner at Biffy's or the Gran Italia and sat at the tables outside on the floor of the Galleria. The waiters came in and out and there were people going by and candles with shades on the table-cloths and... George, the head-waiter, saved us a table. He was a fine waiter and we let him order the meal while we looked at the people, and the great galleria in the dusk, and each other' (Ernest Hemingway, *A Farewell to Arms*, 1928).

Ernest Hemingway convalesced after he was wounded in the Battle of the Piave River in the First World War. And it appears with its cafes in many scenes of the great novel *A Farewell to Arms*.

Another war is intertwined, and much more tragically, with the history of this city space. The bombings of the Allies over Milan on the nights of 13, 15 and 16 August 1943, which claimed 500 lives, destroyed both sides of Via Silvio Pellico and Via Ugo Foscolo, but could not eliminate the citizens' desire to rebuild their Galleria as splendid as before.

In peacetime Italy, the Galleria hosted concerts, catwalks for fashion shows and carnivals, stages for ballets, artistic performances and proclamations of all kinds, as well as the entire caravan of the Giro d'Italia, with all its gatherings of singing and shouting fans. And everyone always has a glass or a cup in their hands, because it is here that the tradition of the aperitif and of *Milano da bere* ('Milan to drink') originally took shape, a label that was applied to the city in the 1980s and still remains.

Milan's association with drinking began in 1867, the very year that the Galleria was inaugurated. It was on 14 November in this year that Gaspare Campari opened the café that bears his name, on the corner of Piazza Duomo. This 'cocktail alchemist' distilled and blended liqueurs in a basement to obtain the original *bitter all'uso d'Hollanda* ('bitter for Dutch use'), dyed carmine red with cochineal and combined with absinthe, gentian, rhubarb, flowers and citrus fruits. Campari had emerged into the world! In 1915, its sister café, 'Camparino', was opened by the son's founder on the other side of the Galleria, a bar with a spectacular Art Nouveau counter, on which cordials and bitters began to be poured in quantity while Davide Campari, Gaspare's son, created the prototype of a machine that was not only able to make soda automatically but also cut slices of lemon, and thus liven up these Campari aperitifs.

The Galleria's entrance arch was completed in 1877

The Galleria is also the site of Café Biffi, the raison d'être of which, from the outset, was panettone – produced at a rate of 500 cakes a day. Not to mention its competitor Caffè Gnocchi, later renamed Gambrinus Halle, and finally Grand Italia, when Italy declared war on Austria in 1915: both cafés entertained passers-by and dignitaries with music, including jazz, which scandalized the bourgeoisie in the 1920s (leading to jazz being known as 'café-concert'). Opposite the Biffi, the Savini restaurant has stood since 1867 – this is the place that provided a regal setting for *riso al salto* (risotto fried in butter), a form of 'left-overs cooking' before the term had even been invented. It was at the Savini's tables, in various different eras, that Giuseppe Verdi, Maria Callas or Frank Sinatra might be found sipping drinks.

The great restoration of the Galleria, carried out over a period of thirteen months between 2014 and 2015, led to the redevelopment of 14,000 square metres (150,695 square feet) of real estate, restoring that luminosity so typical of Milan in the early days, when it had already begun to be known as a 'museum without doors'.

In 1928, the Motta was opened in the Galleria – this bar became synonymous with panettone, and was the first to demand that customers pay for their drinks in advance, getting their receipt at the till. There was also the Marchesi 1824 pasticceria, bought by the Prada group in 2014. Other major brands (Giorgio Armani, Dior, Gucci, Louis Vuitton, Versace) increasingly used gold signs on a black background. The prolific appearance on social profiles of the tag #galleriavittorioemanuele is primarily due to the impressive renovation work that preceded the 2015 Universal Exhibition. The old 'glass house' is shining like never before, and the whole world knows it!

AN OPEN HOUSE FOR EVERYONE

Carlo Cracco was born in Creazzo (Vicenza) on 8 October 1865. After studying at the Hotelier Institute in Recoaro Terme, he went to Milan to work for Gualtiero Marchesi. He perfected his training at the Meridiana in Garlenda (Savona), alongside Alain Ducasse in Monte Carlo, and then at Alain Senderens in Paris. He was chef at the Enoteca Pinchiorri in Florence, moving on to Gualtiero Marchesi in Franciacorta and, in 1996, he finally opened his own restaurant for the first time as owner: Le Clivie in Piobesi d'Alba, Piedmont. In 2001, he opened the Cracco-Peck in Milan (which by 2007 was known simply as 'Cracco'). In February 2018, the Galleria opened.

'What are you going to do in Milan?', my friends and colleagues remonstrated with me: 'it has nothing to offer gastronomically.' Well, I thought, if the master Gualtiero Marchesi won the first three Michelin stars of Italian cuisine here in 1986, this city must have some merit! I have lived in Milan since 1999. On 8 January 2001, we first opened our doors, on Via Victor Hugo, a few steps from Piazza Duomo. These were formidable years for the kitchen and for our restaurant, which was initially called Cracco-Peck. If you're not a creative person, the Milanese won't even look at you, so we try to have our say every day, working tirelessly to come up with recipes that don't just repeat the tired old Italian stereotypes. However, after seventeen unforgettable years, it was finally time for a change: we were looking for a brighter and more comfortable space – in the Via Hugo headquarters we had been two floors below the street, so we needed a fresh location that was better suited to our new ambitions.

For six months, we checked out several places within the city walls, but the most beautiful spaces don't tend to be offered to us restaurateurs: it's usually considered safer to rent them to fashion houses.
A little disconsolate, we eventually met a man who worked for the municipality. He invited us to visit some of his office spaces in the heart of the Galleria. 'Why not?', I thought. After all, no chef had ever imagined opening an ambitious restaurant in the Salotto di Milano. In the early days, this place so full of history had mainly housed cafés and great craftsmen of fabrics, shoes and hats – a fact that had always struck me. My wife Rosa and I went to look at some places at the back of Via Silvio Pellico, but the spaces they were showing us were a disaster: they had not been occupied for twenty-five years, so everything was totally dilapidated, rubble everywhere, and it was all falling apart. Then we looked out of the window of one of these places, and we could see the Octagon shining under its dome of glass and iron, leaving us open-mouthed. What had at first appeared to be an impossible mission, suddenly, one minute later looked like an opportunity too good to pass up. We decide to bid for this space – and we managed to get it! We immediately started work and, after an interminable sequence of meetings and early mornings, drafts and work, not to mention unforeseen events and bouts of swearing, on 21 February 2018, we served our first meals at 'Cracco in Galleria'.

Did we ever have any doubts about taking over the Galleria location? Of course, continually! But if you like something, then sooner or later you just have to make it your own.

A few years have passed since that day and we are now very well settled in our new home. Of course, this is a dynamic, multifaceted project, always changing, even in terms of the building: after having added the Café in the Galleria and the Restaurant on the first floor to the Sala G. Mengoni event space, as well as the Wine Cellar (Cantina) in the basement, we have recently also created an area of accommodation on the highest floor. Now we have our own set of lodgings, where we can house many of the young people who work with us. These operations are working at a loss, of course, but we always say that it is better to accumulate debts than money! The existence of proper living jobs such as these feeds our romantic, slightly reckless passion every day. Our passion for cooking is a fire that burns regardless of profit, every day giving new shape to a cuisine that is neither Italian nor Milanese, neither classic nor innovative, but simply the product of many different people, all fuelled by the same fervour – people like our chef Luca Sacchi, who has been working with us since he was just nineteen years old: his skills are truly extraordinary, whether we're talking about his management of the guys and the ingredients, his deep curiosity as he updates traditional recipes, or his ability to throw contrasting ingredients together to extract the best from each. There's also the unselfishness and sensitivity in Mattia Mangolini's kitchen, and Alessandro Ruggle's amazing ability to put all the important pieces of the puzzle together. Then, finally, there's Rosa's ability to keep it all light, her cheery smile helping us to keep some sense of proportion, faced with the sometimes excessive formality of the culinary world.

The partnership between Carlo Cracco and Luca Sacchi began in 2007, when Luca was only nineteen years old. As soon as former sous chef Matteo Baronetto left the restaurant, in 2013, Cracco turned unhesitatingly to the boy from Abbiategrasso: 'Now you will do the cooking!'. 'But I'm a pastry chef,' he replied. 'That really doesn't matter'.

Carlo Cracco (Libra). He gets going, thinks later. If he says, 'I've had an idea!', run away. Or resign yourself to the fact that it will keep you occupied for days, months, years. A free spirit and an indomitable traveller, he always says what he thinks... even if sometimes it would be better if he didn't. **Luca Sacchi** (Taurus). Honest? Yes. As tactile as a frying pan, he has opinions on everything, even things he doesn't know. A borderline optimist, he's always right, even when he's wrong.

Mattia Mangolini (Virgo). He's so indecisive that to choose a series on television, he needs advice, a survey, a blessing. But he always asks with style. A living inner critic, he corrects your soul. Generous. **Alessandro Ruggle** (Libra with Virgo rising). Ambitious, serious, determined, he always has a plan. But also a plan B, C, D and a colourful diary. Mysterious, intense and passionate. Swiss precision with built-in anxiety.

Cracco in Galleria is a home that we try to keep open for everyone, every day, with careful attention to detail. It is only when a customer sits down at his empty table that we begin the setting, only then that we pull back the curtain on our view of the Octagon, hand him or her the water glass and napkin, the dinner plate and the underplate. This is our welcome – a front-row seat for the Salotto di Milano!

DREAM-LIKE ARCHITECTURE

Having found our spot in the Galleria, we still had to find the right people to design and realize our ambitious and complex, multistorey project. The architects' task was to turn our dream into reality: to define a place with a strong creative personality, which would also respect the classic style of the Salotto di Milano as a whole. We didn't want the restaurant to be like an alien spacecraft gliding into obscurity; what we wanted was a house in symbiosis with its surroundings. Like a reflection in a lake, we wanted to present a faithful image that was nevertheless tinged with a sense of poetry. Studio Peregalli Sartori is a Milanese institution: Roberto Peregalli and Laura Sartori Rimini are the direct heirs of Renzo Mongiardino, decorator and set designer, and one of the most eclectic personalities of post-World War II Italy. To understand their sheer professionalism, one only has to visit their atelier, a labyrinth hidden in the most secluded streets of the city centre, overflowing with paintings, sculptures and delicate pieces of craftwork – a place bursting with ideas, in which looking and touching are prioritized over computer imaging.

The architects Roberto Peregalli and Laura Sartori Rimini wanted to design the restaurant as if it were a private home, creating a dialogue between classicism and the future, and weaving the two together in a way that was only superficially dissonant. Like the restaurant's kitchen itself, the blend of old and new is simultaneously meticulous and also disruptive.

The Café bar-counter and the seating decorated with Studio Peregalli Sartori's interior designs

Top, the Restaurant's reception room, and above, one of the rooms

On the ground floor, the mosaics recall those of the Galleria, and the lift (elevator) echoes the taste for ironwork, exemplified by Mengoni's own network of designs. Here and there, the distinctive Milan yellow peeps out, but the restaurant's vision goes well beyond the idea of a refined 'philological' exercise, straying into the sphere of invention.

We chose Studio Peregalli Sartori because they design beautiful private houses. The very few restaurants they have designed were conceived primarily as dwellings, places where one did not go just for the pleasure of eating but to immerse oneself, as if one were part of a painting, cocooned in a warm and other-worldly atmosphere. After two years of uninterrupted work, they were able to completely reinvent the nature of a building that had previously housed a neutrally coloured car showroom (on the ground floor) and the offices of the Italian Alpine Club (on the two upper floors). A hundred or so decorators, plasterers, upholsterers, masons and carpenters combined to carve out a space imbued with the essence of Milanese and international elegance. This blend of the local and the global is only superficially contradictory because it is actually consistent with the city's great vocation for openness, always capable of absorbing and giving, learning and teaching in the same measure. With its somewhat understated luxury, the style of the house provides continuity and reinterprets the building within this concoction of entablatures, bas-reliefs, pilasters, mosaics and ironwork that has made Giuseppe Mengoni's Salotto famous throughout the world. There is a strong sense of continuity between inside and outside – a sense of belonging to the city that is reflected in the materials and colours, including the unique Milanese yellow that, according to legend, accidentally dropped from a mosaic in the Duomo to provide the distinctive colour of saffron and marrow risotto, the pièce de resistance of Milanese cuisine.

Architecturally, the Cracco in Galleria is a receptacle of some complexity, containing and projecting images of places and times both near and far.

Above, a detail of the Sala Mengoni, and to the left, one of the rooms in the Restaurant

The carpet creates a muted environment, and the curtains of gilded metal allow the light to filter through while also screening the guests, recreating the ambience of restaurants in the past, where people went to celebrate more intimate occasions.

There is Milan, but there is also the echo of the iron architecture of Paris. There is Europe, but there are also calming hints of the Orient here and there. This is a treasure chest that traverses the ages, starting in the nineteenth century, spanning the 1920s and 1940s and eventually arriving at the present day. Even the 'present' is not solely confined to today: one of the most important objectives was to build a restaurant that would age well, with an architectural concept deliberately intended to last over time, as we see with the most successful French 'maisons' beyond the Alps. Cracco in Galleria is a timeless project – not only the most beautiful restaurant *in* the city but also inextricably linked *with* the city. Our dream soars upwards through four storeys, each marked by quite different aesthetic influences.

CRACCO
CRACCO
CRACCO

CAFÉ

If you enter Galleria Vittorio Emanuele II through the triumphal arch of the Piazza Duomo, just before you reach the Ottagono, you'll find on the left a terrace area covered and semi-enclosed by glass, brass and plants across the length of three shop windows, each of which is surmounted by the word Cracco. This is the ground-floor Café, welcoming you to our world: our own 'salon' within the wider Salotto of the Galleria. The architects' intention was that the Café would create continuity between inside and outside, with its widespread references to the style of Giuseppe Mengoni, designer of the Galleria: the hand-painted walls, the mosaics, the arches, the stuccoes dividing the walls from the ceiling, the marble floor – all of these provide an internal evocation of the materials and colours that dominate the rest of the Galleria, under its iron and glass roof. On the other hand, the interior also recalls the motifs of a turn-of-the-century Milanese café, with its antique mirrors, frames and shelves, while the long bar counter, and the smaller one next to it, were both tracked down in a Parisian brothel. The entrance to the Café has been deliberately designed to create an immediate impact to which no one can remain indifferent. An urgent invitation to travel is summoned up by the Liberty-style lift (elevator), a veritable iron and faux-bronze spacecraft brooding

The Café's breakfast includes plain or filled Italian croissants, pain au chocolats, puff pastries, plain or filled Venetian pastries, puff pastries, berry pastries, apple croissants and pistachio and sour cherry pastries

Top, mirrors, frames, shelves, walls: every piece of furniture seeks to evoke the architectural motifs of late-19th-century Milanese cafés.

Bottom, there's even a vintage counter discovered in a Parisian brothel.

The Café warmly embraces all those who walk through the Galleria. We extend this same convivial and unrestrained welcome to everyone.

over the left-hand side of the café like some kind of elaborate strong box – a vehicle ready to launch you into orbit. The Café is a space open to all, providing the most 'democratic' welcome possible, and issuing a cheery good morning to tourists and office workers, bankers and workers, shop assistants and artisans, all happy to stop by and order coffee and croissants at affordable prices. But this is also a place to spend time at any hour of the day, from morning until late at night: it's up to you to choose between breakfast, lunch, afternoon tea, pre-dinner aperitif, dinner or after-dinner. For this reason, the Café is probably our most complex challenge, tackling the tricky brief of intertwining countertop pastries and full-scale meals – two quite different offerings. Since the very beginning of our adventure, we've invested a lot of time and resources in the pastries, and today we are happy to serve brioches made by our own pastry chefs, in a kitchen just above the dining area: the only café to offer this in the very heart of Milan. At lunch and dinner, on the other hand, the Café's aim is to prepare traditional Milanese and Italian dishes, all well-made but also updated with fresh touches and modern-day discernment. Dishes such as saffron risotto with grilled (broiled) marrow or veal ossobuco and gremolada are mainstays of Milanese cuisine from time immemorial, but we strive to give them a contemporary spin, consistent with the tastes and needs of today's customers. This is also our approach to very Italian specialities such as 'spaghetti al pomodoro', transformed from the basic ingredients by talented artisans. Even our pizza tries to be tastier and more appetizing than pure tradition dictates. Essentially, we think of the Café as providing a 'smarter offer' than the Restaurant upstairs. It's our completely distinctive way of reaching out not only to Milanese citizens but to tourists from all over the world.

SAVINI

ITALIAN CORNETTO

Whether you eat it plain or filled with apricot jam, vanilla or chocolate cream, the highlight of any flying breakfast for those who pass through the Galleria in the morning sunshine is our Italian-style cornetto. This is a white flaky butter pastry, blending eggs with enticing flavours, giving off the scents of citrus and vanilla. It is a coveted item, not least because it is has only half the volume of the traditional ‘brioche’, although it is often wrongly described as a brioche in northern Italy. Compared to the French croissant, the cornetto is a softer and less unctuous pastry, less fragrant but more flavoursome – a kind of culinary reflection of the anthropological differences between the Italians and the French. Food historians agree that the croissant and cornetto share a common ancestor: the ‘kipfel’, a crescent-shaped pastry that Austrian bakers invented to celebrate victory over the Ottomans in 1683, the year that the latter tried, and failed, to conquer Vienna. Given the intensive trade relations between the Austro-Hungarian Empire and the Venetian Republic, the kipfel – comprising flour, butter, sugar, eggs and sometimes ground almonds and marzipan – spread gradually southwards, morphing into endless variations that today rule out any strict classifications. Curiously enough, the ‘treccia with raisins and chocolate’ (a kind of plaited/braided loaf), another popular breakfast item, also has the same roots as the cornetto: it is the Italian take on the Austrian ‘kranz’, a long, narrow leavened speciality plaited with buttery puff pastry. There is also a popular southern variant – a treccia combined with zibibbo raisins, Calabrian liquorice and candied orange peel. The croissants and plaited breads – the two constants of the Italian breakfast – lie at the heart of a whole range of limited-edition specials, for which people can be seen queuing up even before the Café opens: the three-chocolate ‘corallina’, the ‘dischetti’ with strawberry and elderberry cream, the ‘pain suisse’ with peanuts and caramel, the pain au chocolat (both classic and with added coconut), the caramel and amaretto and pistachio and orange kranz. Ingredients and traditions, often travelling from distant worlds, find their natural home in our oven.

Bread, butter and jam

BREAD, BUTTER AND JAM

Is there a combination that defines the Italian breakfast better than bread, butter and jam? In the Italian countryside, the custom of placing a piece of cheese on top of a piece of bread is lost in the mists of time. Later, they also added small pieces of fresh fruit, preferably very ripe, and crushed with their own hands. Some far-sighted grandmothers took the ensemble to its logical conclusion with the addition of sugar, cinnamon and other spices.

We take these age-old wisdoms and update them with today's raw materials and techniques: a good Alpine-style 'malga butter' (which was once a luxury) and a knife to spread it on a slice of bread. Very little sugar is needed because the natural sweetness of apricots, peaches or cherries that we pick from our countryside is enough. These humble ingredients can punch above their weight to create a full, natural flavour: haute cuisine, early in the morning.

VENEZIANA BRIOCHES

Despite its name, Veneziana is a Milanese speciality, a posh descendant of 'fugassa', the rustic, dry dough from the Veneto region that our ancestors loved to dunk in milk. Veneziana used to be mainly eaten during the festivities following Christmas, but nowadays it's considered far too good to be consumed only seasonally. It's a leavened dough made of butter, flour, sugar and eggs, like panettone, but generally without candied fruit. We fill it with custard and top it with almond icing (frosting) and sugar crystals. With both filling and topping we try to be very generous.

Veneziana brioches

APPLE TARTS

Apfelstrudel, tarte aux pommes, torta di mele – is there a dessert more popular than apple tart? In Italy it's much more than a delicacy – it's a ritual ingrained in the habits of every family. It began as a clever way of using up shrivelled or bruised fruit, but it quickly became a universal comfort food, a taste that still reminds us of Sundays when we were kids, and when people went to shops in search of the best slice of tart.

We prepare it at the weekend, as it traditionally always was, and we try to give it a good, cosy, familiar look. Technically, it is not actually that simple or intuitive to prepare because we make a pastry that is relatively high in buckwheat, baked with a press in the centre. The large, melting pieces of apple fruit (different kinds of apple, but all from Trentino) are immersed in a natural jelly, with a layer of very thick purée. These are modern culinary tricks, but we try to apply them as unobtrusively as possible. So that everyone can just tuck into their slice of tart, with no questions asked.

RECIPES
FROM THE CAFÉ

Italian Cornetto

Makes 865 g paton to get 12–14 Cornetti, each 60 g raw

400 g **very strong white flour** (W index 360–390), plus extra for dusting
90 g **sourdough starter** after first feeding (24°C/32°F)
7 g **dried yeast**
25 g **skimmed milk powder**
60 g **egg yolk**
54 g **demerara (turbinado) sugar**
5 g **acacia honey**
9 g **salt**
1 **vanilla pod (bean)**, split in half lengthways and seeds scraped out
65 g **unsalted butter 82% fat** (4°C/39°F), cut into cubes
200 g **unsalted butter 82% fat**, for laminating
155 ml **water**

FOR THE EGG WASH
20 ml **milk**
10 g **egg yolk**

FOR THE GLAZE (AFTER BAKING)
25 ml **water**
12 g **fine caster (superfine) sugar**
zest of ½ orange (optional)

Grease a 60 x 40-cm (50 x 16-inch) baking tray with butter. Mix the flour, sourdough starter, yeast, milk powder, water and egg yolk in a mixer fitted with a dough hook for 6 minutes, or until a dough is formed. Add the sugar and honey and continue to knead for 6 minutes. Add the salt, vanilla seeds and the butter cubes and knead for 10–12 minutes until fully incorporated. The resulting dough should be at a temperature no higher than 25–27°C/77–81°F. Gather the dough into a ball by rotating and lightly compacting it, then place it on the prepared tray. Allow the dough to rest for 40 minutes, uncovered (a skin should form), then roll it out into a rectangle the same size as the tray. Cover with baking parchment and allow to rest at 4°C/39°F for 12 hours.
After the dough has rested, roll out the butter for laminating to a 6-mm/¼-inch thickness. Turn the dough over so that the skin is underneath, then roll out the dough on a lightly floured surface to a thickness of about 1.5 cm/⅝ inch. Encase the butter in the dough, then make one book fold, followed by one letter fold. Allow to rest for about 30 minutes at 4°C/39°F. Roll out the laminated dough on a lightly floured surface to about 50 x 90–100-cm/20 x 35½–39-inch wand, about a 0.4 mm/⅙ inch thickness. Cut out 8-cm-/3¼-inch-wide strips, then cut the strips on the diagonal to form triangles and roll them up as if making croissants. Allow the cornetti to prove at 26–27°C/79–81°F for about 2 hours. Preheat the oven to 180°C/350°F. For the egg wash, mix the egg yolk and milk together in a small bowl, then brush over the top of the cornetti. Bake in the oven for 18–21 minutes. For the glaze, boil the water with the syrup. To glaze, brush the cornetti while still hot with the syrup.

Bread, butter and jam

Makes 2 loaves of 1 kg each

FOR THE WHITE BREAD
400 g **semolina**
200 g **spelt flour**
400 g **strong white flour** (W index 280–350), plus extra for dusting
10 g **caster (superfine) sugar**
610 ml **water**
200 g **fresh yeast**
0.5 g **liquid sourdough starter**
25 g **salt**
100 ml **water**

TO SERVE
unsalted butter
peach, apricot or persimmon jam

Mix the flours, sugar, the 610 g water, the yeast and liquid sourdough starter together in a mixer fitted with a dough hook until it forms a smooth dough. Turn off the mixer and allow the dough to rest in the bowl for 40 minutes. Add the salt and the 100 g water to the dough and knead for 20 minutes, then allow to rest for 40 minutes. Turn the dough out onto a lightly floured work surface and spread into a rectangle. Fold it into thirds (letter fold) and rest again for 40 minutes. Repeat the folding and resting operation twice more, then shape the dough into loaves and prove in the fridge at 4–6°C/39°F for 12 hours. Preheat oven to 250°C/482°F upper temperature and 235°C/255°F lower temperature. Bake for 40 minutes for a 1-kg loaf and for 25 minutes for a 500-g loaf. Cut the bread into 1.5-cm-/⅝-inch-thick slices and toast until golden, then allow to cool on a wire rack to room temperature. Serve with unsalted butter and peach, apricot or persimmon jam according to preference and season.

VISTAMARE JAMS
Peaches, apricots and persimmons are the fruits used to make the jams that are served for breakfast at the Café. These jams are made using high-pressure technology and a low percentage of cane sugar to allow the aromatic and acidic flavours of the fruit to remain intact.

Veneziana brioches

Makes 12 brioches

100 g **unsalted butter**, cut into cubes, plus extra for greasing
335 g **strong white flour** (W index 320)
85 g **liquid sourdough starter**
6 g **fresh yeast**
40 ml **milk**
165 g **egg**
45 g **caster (superfine) sugar**
22 g **acacia honey**
6 g **salt**
½ **vanilla pod (bean)**, split in half lengthways and seeds scraped out
nibbed sugar, for sprinkling

FOR THE ICING
50 g **farina di mandorle (ground almonds)**
100 g **fine caster (superfine) sugar**
50 g **cornflour (cornstarch)**
50 g **egg whites**
0.2 g **salt**
50 g **sunflower oil**
10 g **baking powder**

Grease a baking tray with butter. Mix the flour, sourdough starter, yeast, milk and egg in a stand mixer fitted with a paddle attachment for 5 minutes, or until a dough is formed. Add the sugar and honey and knead for a further 5 minutes. Add the salt, vanilla seeds and butter cubes and knead until fully incorporated. Gather the dough into a ball by rotating it and compacting it well, then place it on the prepared baking tray. Cover with a cloth and allow to rest at room temperature for 30–40 minutes. Divide the dough into 65-g portions. Using your hands, shape each portion of dough into a ball by rotating and compacting it. Allow to rest for 10 minutes, then rotate and compact each ball again. Allow the brioches to prove at 26–27°C/79–81°F for 2½ hours. Preheat the oven to 200°C/400°F. Meanwhile, prepare the icing. Whisk all the ingredients in a stand mixer fitted with a whisk for 2 minutes (without whipping), then transfer the mixture to a piping (pastry) bag. Pipe a spiral of icing on the top of the risen brioches, then sprinkle with nibbed sugar and bake for about 15 minutes. Allow to cool on a wire rack.

Apple tarts

Makes about 18 tarts

350 g **strong white flour** (W index 280–350), plus extra for dusting
150 g **buckwheat flour**
75 g **caster (superfine) sugar**
25 g **acacia honey**
100 g **whole egg**
75 g **egg yolk**
75 ml **milk**
125 g **unsalted butter**, softened, plus extra for greasing
50 g **apple sauce**
10 g **salt**
25 g **fresh yeast**
150 g **unsalted butter**, for laminating
Pastry cream (see page 253), to serve

Mix the flours, sugar, honey, eggs, yolks and milk together in a stand mixer on medium speed until the liquids are fully incorporated and a dough forms. Cover the bowl with cling film (plastic wrap) and allow the dough to rest for 1 hour. Lightly grease a baking tray. Mix 50 g of the softened butter with the apple sauce and salt in a bowl until combined, then set aside. Add the yeast to the dough and mix on high speed until the dough comes away from the sides of the bowl. Add the remaining 75 g softened butter, a third at a time, until the dough is smooth, elastic and a little glossy. Incorporate the butter, salt and apple mixture into the dough, then roll out the dough on the greased tray into a 1-cm-/½-inch-thick rectangle. Chill in the freezer at -18°C/-0.4°F for 1 hour, then refrigerate for 12 hours. Roll out the 150 g butter for laminating into a rectangle, encase it in the dough and make three letter folds. Then roll out the dough on a lightly floured surface to 7–8 mm/⅜ inch thickness and roll it up into a long cylinder. Chill in the freezer at -20°C/-4°F for 1 hour, then slice into 1-cm-/½-inch-thick discs weighing 50–60 g each. Place the discs on a lightly greased baking tray, cover and allow to rise at 26–28°C/79–82°F.

FOR THE APPLE FILLING
350 g **apples**, diced
75 g **caster (superfine) sugar**
50 ml **double (heavy) cream**
½ **vanilla pod (bean)**, split in half lengthways and seeds scraped out
20 g **sugar**
5 g **pectin NH**
apricot glaze, for brushing

Preheat the oven to 150°C/325°F. Arrange the diced apples on a large baking sheet and dry out in the oven for 15 minutes. Cook the caster (superfine) sugar to a caramel and stop the cooking process with the cream and vanilla seeds. Mix the 20 g sugar and pectin together in a small bowl, then add to the caramel with the warm apples and cook for 15 minutes over a medium heat until creamy. Spoon the filling into 5-cm-/2-inch-diameter moulds. Allow to cool, then freeze until chilled.

To assemble, lay each dough disc in a 6.5 x 2-cm/2½ x ¾-inch silicone mould with micro holes. Prove at room temperature for about 90 minutes. Preheat the oven to 180°C/350°F. Using a 5-cm-/2-inch-diameter dough stamp, press a cavity in the centre of the dough. Spread a tablespoon of pastry cream inside the cavity and fill with a frozen apple filling disc. Bake in the oven for 14–15 minutes. Quickly cool the tarts in a blast chiller before unmoulding. Brush with apricot glaze.

RISTORANTE

After our lift (elevator) launches off from the ground floor, it changes its appearance on every floor. On the first floor, it casts off the iron and faux-bronze guise of the Café, and enters a 'parallelepiped' or cuboid, inlaid with mirror and metal, ushering guests into our reception hall. This is only the beginning of the adventure in Cracco in Galleria, but we cherish this prologue because, if you can get the introduction right, the rest of the story flows like a dream.

The first steps out of the lift are accompanied by the traditional creaking of the parquet floor: after a long restoration programme, we managed to preserve the original materials laid by Mengoni himself, then we used some of the surviving fabric to 'plug' even the most ruined parts of the restaurant, an operation of which we are truly proud.

The ceiling of the reception room has been restored to its original geometric patterns and colours, while the walls and doors have been embellished with grey-blue woodwork. All around, the walls are lined with hand-painted wallpaper decorated with oriental-style floral friezes, including an arrangement of ikebana cut branches stretching into the distance and instilling a vision of nature within the four walls. This is the colourful, luminous prologue to the Restaurant.

APERITIF AT THE FUMOIR

As you slip through the little door at the Fumoir, a mini-lounge opens up in front of you, transporting you back to the Milan of fifty years ago. Here you are in a very different setting, and you may feel as if you have entered a secluded oasis. The air you breathe, however, is just the same as on the other floors.

The creaking of the parquet floor in the reception room is muted by the restaurant's carpeting, but the sound creates a special, very intimate ambience. This takes us into the Fumoir, an island of tranquillity with its own distinct aesthetics, and a private space in which diners can be genuinely pampered.

The Fumoir is a small art-deco room with a mahogany and zinc bar-counter. Three seats are set along the counter, with glittering displays behind. The walls of the Fumoir are covered in a moss-green metallic mesh, and a few side tables are scattered around. This is somewhere to enjoy a peaceful after-dinner liqueur or a magnificent cigar. Alternatively, even before dinner, a small menu is available here, including our most famous dish, and several other specialities that have featured in the Restaurant's tasting menus. In the Fumoir, these amuse-bouches can truly bask in their own glory – usually only one or two bites, these tempting morsels can ease you into the general ambience of our cuisine.

CARAMELIZED RUSSIAN SALAD

From the moment that caramelized Russian salad first appeared in the royal courts of Italy and France in the sixteenth century, through to its adoption in Piedmont – and of course the version created by Lucien Olivier, the Russian chef after whom the speciality is said to be named – it would take a whole book to tell the story of the journey of this salad across time and space. This is a truly transnational speciality that has become a very popular starter (appetizer) or side dish at our tables. The caramelized Russian salad is the one dish we have not been able to take off the menu since the day it first came on, in 2001.

The distinctive taste of our Russian salad is very much a question of quantity: the combination of ingredients seemed to us to have a flaw, with the salad becoming a little cloying to the palate after the first spoonful. Hence our idea of serving just 30 grams (about 1 ounce) at the beginning of the meal, after having cooked all of its ingredients separately: potatoes, carrots, peas, green beans, salted and dried capers, without mustard and with vinegar and lemon, and a measured dose of white mayonnaise, as tradition dictates. We enclose all of these things between two discs of isomalt – a sugar substitute – sealed with a blowtorch just before serving.

The composition and preparation of this sweet and salty dish has not changed in over twenty years. What has changed, however, is the presentation: for a long time, the dish was placed in the rectangular slot of a black polyethylene holder. At Cracco in Galleria, we have opted for a version that is more consistent with the style of the new restaurant, so the salad is now placed in the curved slot of a gilded semicircle, raised on copper feet and engraved with the arches of the Milanese designer Gio Ponti, an important symbol for us. This is a timeless taste, which customers always ask for, and we are happy to oblige.

Tongue terrine in a brioche crust

Nori, veal tongue and date

TONGUE TERRINE IN A BRIOCHE CRUST

With their opulent shapes, their bright geometry and colours, and the sense of festivity they create at the centre of the table, terrines in the classic French tradition have always exerted an intense fascination for us. Often, however, their beauty may not be matched by a worthy taste. For this terrine recipe, we decided that it may not be the most beautiful in the world, but it certainly had to be good.

In defining its taste, we decided to work on a great classic of northern Italian cuisine, 'il bollito' (boiled meat), in other words boiled cuts of meat and vegetables. We chose veal tongue, cutting it very finely and serving it in a millefeuille form, alternating the layers of tongue with layers of pear mostarda, fresh pear, black truffle and slices of cooked 'lardo' (cured pork fat). We wrap the terrine in Swiss chard leaves and surround this parcel with a raw brioche dough, baking it in the oven. The terrine is then left to cool, and finally sliced so that it can be served with a fresh pear and spicy mustard cream. A perfect Italian terrine.

NORI, VEAL TONGUE AND DATE

In this dish, our initial aim was to elaborate on the centuries-old Italian tradition of boiled meat, traditionally combined with opulent, musty sauces. The veal tongue with candied chinotto mustard and cumin comes from here and is paired with a date purée, shallot vinegar and white pepper, a trio of ingredients very dear to Alain Senderens, the unforgettable Nouvelle Cuisine chef at Lucas Carton, who presided over an important stage in the young Carlo Cracco's apprenticeship. Below the tongue, we add the crispy exoticism of a nori seaweed, brushed with buckwheat and rice and then puffed in oil. Four strong bites, with distant references, but an unmistakably Italian flavour.

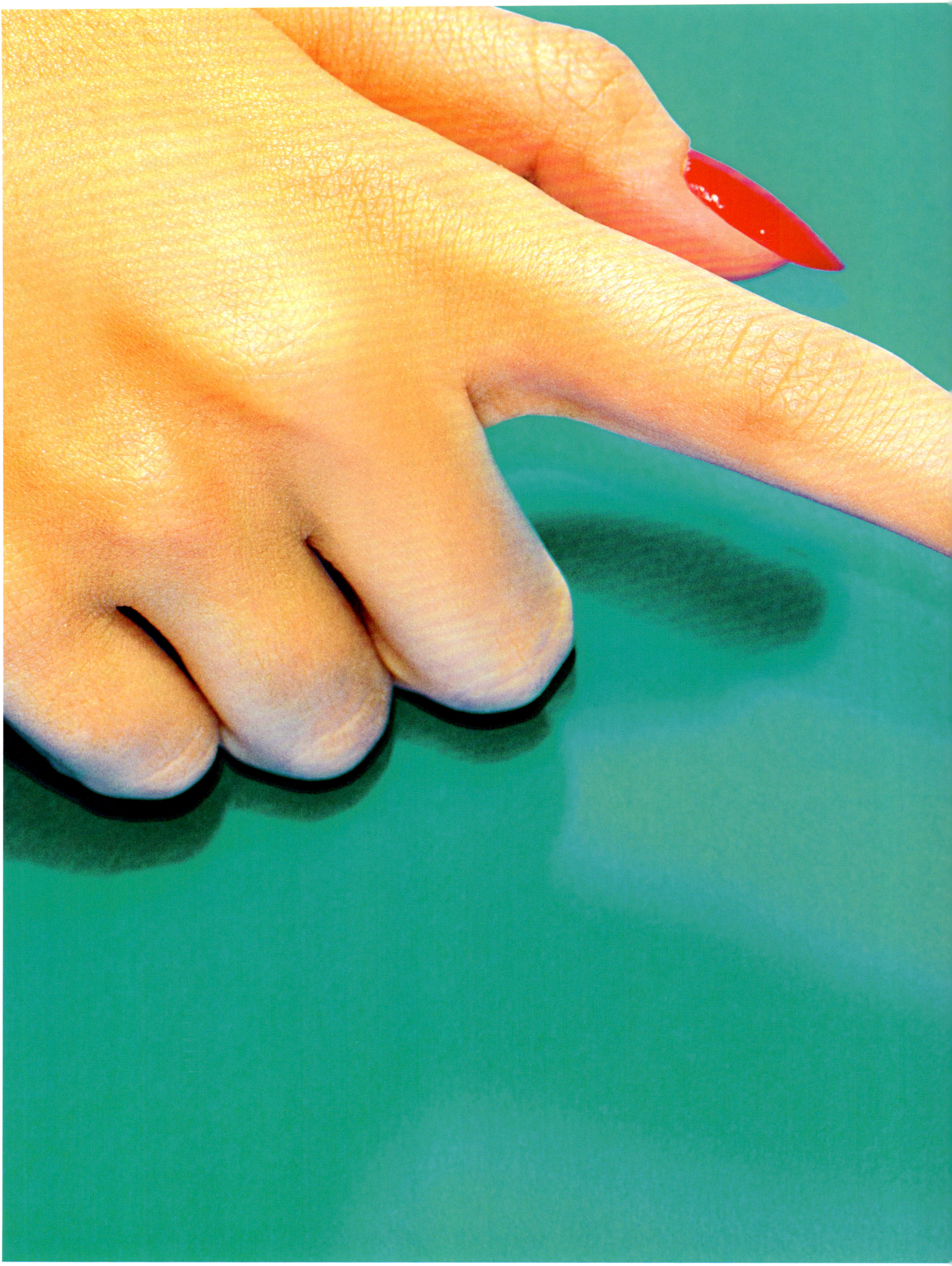

Soft saffron buns, gold and caviar

SOFT SAFFRON BUNS, GOLD AND CAVIAR

A small taste, with multiple meanings. The first is the work on soft textures that we have been doing for a long time, such as those of a pan brioche, a milk bread or a simple Italian bread. We try to assign strong flavours to these, to be concentrated in two or three bites at the most. For this taste, we focused on the sweet and sour notes of a savoury saffron custard, a technique traditionally applied to sweet ingredients. We have combined two noble and precious elements: the savoury counterbalance of caviar, also in the form of butter, and an edible gold leaf. Gold, saffron, caviar: come to think of it, these are ingredients made famous by Gualtiero Marchesi, the unforgettable master of Italian cuisine. An unconscious homage, telling of his ever-living influence.

CRISPY RICE CRACKERS

These crispy rice crackers (or 'rice chips'), appearing as a kind of interlude in the Fumoir or an amuse-bouche at the table, have long been served in our restaurants. And presumably they will continue to be served, given their popularity and their potentially endless variations. The basic technique is the same as for standard puffed rice, but instead of working on the individual grains, we work with a mass of whisked boiled rice, roll it into sheets, dry it and puff it up in boiling oil.

Tomatoes, seaweed, spinach, mushrooms, polenta, capers, anchovies... there are about thirty varieties that we make, but the number is potentially infinite because, in addition to the seasoning, the chosen rice (white, purple or black, wild or basmati) can also vary. Our favourites? Saffron, basmati rice, buckwheat and beetroot, with anchovies, tomato and oregano. The rice sheets never come alone because we always serve them with seasonal fried food, such as pumpkin flowers, borage, sage or shiso...

Crispy rice crackers

DINING

For us, creativity is making the good taste better. It is never a manifestation of any genius or talent, but simply the premise for a new beginning, a mere suggestion that can be completed by others.

A patterned carpet ushers customers into the actual restaurant. This is divided into three main rooms and two small private rooms, with each of the rooms separated from the other by double doors opening onto decorations of pilasters in bas-relief, arches framing mirrors in ochre and green tones and curtains of gilded metal fabric lining the spaces discretely and calmly. The design is intended to reproduce the intimacy of one's own home, with low lights diffused by wall sconces and lampshades, such as the transparent-stemmed lamps on the table, a tribute to the aesthetics of the eternal Chez Maxim's in Paris. The great Milanese designer Giò Ponti is the primary inspiration for the sober green and red velvets, the orange of the seats and the colours of the plates, their overall harmony characterized by an awed tranquillity, gently vying with the beauty of the Galleria's Octagon, visible in all its majesty beyond the window of the most coveted table.

We do our best to actively disobey the rules of the kind of perfect cooking that is always correctly measured down to the millimetre, and never strays outside the circle of perfection. Instead, we're more interested in the performance itself, the stimulation of personal growth, and the expression of the individual skills of each cook and waiter.

At Cracco in Galleria, we strive every day to intertwine hospitality and cuisine, history and the avant-garde, Milan and the world beyond. This is in many ways the natural consequence of Carlo Cracco's personal narrative, a journey that has criss-crossed the Veneto region, France, Piedmont and Lombardy over the decades. Since opening our restaurant in the Galleria in February 2018, our focus has increasingly been on Milan and the region to which it belongs, not least because of the origins of our chef Luca Sacchi. These are cooking traditions that are historically rustic, but simultaneously quite elevated, mainly because they are so full of ingenuity: whether in the countryside or in the city, the daily effort has always been to build happy flavours with ingredients of humble extraction, a basic premise that we try to hang onto. In our menus, you'll find that 'luxury' raw materials are carefully apportioned; for us, it is a much more stimulating challenge to dream up tasty dishes using meat from farmyard animals, unused cuts, wild herbs and offal, stale bread, frogs or snails. This is the challenge that we face in our cooking, with the wide variety of resources and textures that we have been working with for a long time. These dishes are in a state of constant evolution; they may be expressions of Lombardian peasant cuisine, but we seek constantly to elaborate on them, drawing on techniques from faraway countries while always sticking close to the histories of our own familiar places. We are above all concerned with the essence of each of our dishes rather than perfect aesthetics. This is because we have always believed that the beauty of cooking lies in what you taste much more than what you see.

MARINATED EGG YOLK

When asked to name our favourite ingredient, we always answer 'the egg'. This ancient symbol of rebirth and fertility is a fundamental presence in kitchens around the world, and one of the main pillars of Italian cuisine – just think of the importance of fresh pasta. Such is our fascination with this ingredient that 'eggs' have long been a separate course on our menu, independent of starters (appetizers), main courses or desserts. This is because we have always tried to transform them from the inside out, but above all we have tried to move them outside the mainstream, considering their infinite possibilities.

Fried, fondant or soft-boiled: we have transformed the egg into so many different textures but the style that appeals to us most is the marinated egg. Separating the white from the yolk and soaking the latter in salt and sugar is a cooking method with Asian roots, since it was the Chinese and Japanese who first realized that chicken eggs could be marinated in the same way as fish eggs. At Cracco in Galleria, we have tried to do even more to enhance this yolk that has been solidified by changing the nature of its proteins, transforming it from a simple ingredient into the central element of a dish. Adding a purée of beans boiled in water to the recipe gives it an even softer and creamier texture. Over time, the marinated egg yolk has gone far beyond our original intentions and has become a versatile, cross-cutting ingredient in a substantial number of other dishes: today we can use it in its *natural* state, candied or fried, as a pastry, spaghetti or ravioli, grated in the manner of a botargo (mullet or tuna roe delicacy) or even whisked into a risotto. To emphasize its centrality in our menu, we serve it even before a customer has given their order.

Marinated yolk butter is our version of the salted spreadable butter provided at the start of a meal, a kind of 'salsa cocktail' without mayonnaise, but with more richness and flavour. We bring it to the table immediately, setting it next to the extra-virgin olive oil. Customers like it so much that some even ask for it four times during the same meal.

Marinated egg yolk

TOMATO, MOZZARELLA AND BASIL

Tomato, mozzarella and basil. It's a very Italian blend of ingredients, not only because of the combination of colours recalling our flag, nor even because these are the key constituents of the margherita, the most popular pizza. At the beginning of the millennium, we took up the Catalan master Ferran Adrià's invitation to explore novel textures using familiar ingredients. This is why, over twenty years ago, our first version of the recipe was already based on tomato gel, cubes of buffalo mozzarella and crisp basil leaves. Over time, this recipe has evolved in various ways: we have added candied, cooked confit, concentrated the tomato even more, turned the mozzarella into a 'foam' and scattered basil in the crispy corolla of the rim. We have also added capers, dried anchovies and oregano. This is a brand new perspective on classic Italy.

Everyday salad

EVERYDAY SALAD

In the Lombardy countryside, between the two world wars, it was not uncommon for farmers to have their crops and livestock confiscated from one day to the next. But this was no time to despair: alternatives had to be found immediately, and any leftover food had to be reused. This gave rise to very basic, tasty dishes such as 'ravanei e ton': an everyday salad combining canned tuna, stale bread and radish leaves. At the restaurant, we took this as our starting point, and instead of tuna, we used palamita (also known as bonito), an oily mackerel-like fish, which we moulded into little spheres resembling radishes. We then combined the palamita balls with such things as herbs, shallot cream and even caviar because it is important to enhance every little expression of what we might call pure 'hunger gastronomy'. This is an idea that derives from the very roots of Italian cuisine.

SEA SALAD WORLD TOUR

We've always loved the 'sea salad', a great Italian and Mediterranean classic, too often debased by endless bland copies. This recipe is a version of our 'marinara in sfoglie' (seaside in wafers), a dish we have been making for a long time. It consists of a paste of blended seafood (prawns/shrimp, scallops, blackened cuttlefish and octopus), rolled into thin sheets and baked in the oven to produce our seafood wafers. The difference nowadays is that the ingredients come from three continents: there is not only a South American snapper ceviche (with lemon and anchovy drippings), but also a thickened broth of herbs from northern Europe (mountain pine, aniseed, fennel, celery, dill...) and a yuzu jelly from Asia. We wanted to convey the pleasure of experiencing raw fish with all of its potent acidic and saline components, blending together the artisanal products of several distant climes.

Sea Salad World Tour

CANNELLINI BEANS, SEA URCHINS AND TARRAGON

Fish and legumes is a combination deeply rooted in Italian cuisine, even before the great Tuscan chef Fulvio Pierangelini created his classic 'passatina di ceci con gamberi' (chickpea soup with prawns/shrimp) in the 1980s. This dish begins with the age-old culinary dialogue between the Mediterranean sea and the land, which in our case intertwines the noble elegance of a cannellini bean purée with the meaty savouriness of sea urchins, an ingredient that for us is almost an obsession. This recipe includes a special note – well-hidden at the base of the dish – that breaks up the flavours and completes the overall feel of the dish: cream of calf's liver, a buttery, iron-rich blend topped with the rich aroma of tarragon oil. From the bottom upwards, your spoon takes you on a journey through beautifully contrasting tastes and textures.

Lombard-style frog soup and fried frogs

LOMBARD-STYLE FROG SOUP AND FRIED FROGS

Although they are generally less frequently consumed nowadays, frogs have historically played an important role in the cuisine of the Lower Lombardy region. 'Eat the haunch... and eat the bones too', our mother used to say, after our father had come home with a basket full of frogs caught in ditches and ponds. As children, we were especially fond of two recipes: frog stew – made by browning whole frogs in white wine, then mashing them – and simple fried frogs. In our recipe, we have tried to merge these two traditional dishes together, with a few clever updates thrown in. We add buffalo ricotta cheese to the soup, following the same logic with which cheese has been added to other soups, just to create a little extra surprise and comfort. Then we combine the soup with braised frogs, having prepared these rather like creamed cod, rolling the croquette balls in a crumb of rice and dried pork rind. Out of this meticulous preparation emerges a mouthful of pure fried frog, which can be munched bonelessly, with a well-seasoned broth to bring out the flavour. This is 'total frog', which starts from the basics, but achieves something like the sophistication of a great twentieth-century French velouté. All of this is combined into a light and voluptuous whole, as contemporary taste demands.

OYSTERS AND LARDO

Tradition is the main starting point for all of our recipes, but sometimes the spark can be generated simply by something we habitually do in the restaurant. We have played for a long time with the intertwining of the oyster and the pronounced notes of fig or buffalo mozzarella, combinations seemingly without any link to the past. In this case, the interplay is between pig and oyster, a cheeky match that we owe to the genius of the Spanish chef Ferran Adrià. Here, oyster and lardo are both steamed and then rolled together into a ball that combines the fatty and the viscous, the iodine and the meaty. This results in a kind of quenelle, tempered by the sweetness of a fresh persimmon purée – an ingredient we love – and finished off with tarragon oil and baked walnuts.

Oysters and lardo

Surf and turf: crayfish, mushrooms and catmint oil

SURF AND TURF: CRAYFISH, MUSHROOMS AND CATMINT OIL

The spark for this dish was lit by our chef Luca Sacchi's first cooking experience, when he worked at Nico il Tarantino, a battle-hardened restaurant on the Vigevanese, a busy artery linking Milan and Alessandria. Nico's signature dish was the 'bis di primi' (double servings of a starter): side by side on the same plate, a generous portion of seafood rice as well as a serving of porcini mushroom rice, leaving the lucky recipient to jump back and forth endlessly between the two dishes.
On closer inspection, crustaceans and mushrooms are not an odd couple in Italian traditional cuisine: some late nineteenth-century cookbooks already combined these two glorious expressions of land and sea, a juxtaposition that has gradually become quintessentially Italian.
Our classic 'surf and turf' consists of a crayfish sauce enriched by plump prataioli button mushrooms. Each serving comes with three tablespoons of this bisque with its very pronounced sweet-and-sour earthy smell. The dish is topped by slices of blanched porcini mushrooms, crayfish tails and an oil prepared from catmint leaves.

SOFT PLANKTON BUNS AND MUSTARD CAVIAR

This is another 'soft bites' dish *(see also Soft squash buns and trout on page 104)*, using soft pieces of strongly flavoured Italian 'seasoned bread', to be eaten in two or three bites. In this instance, the inspiration is one of the most iconic recipes from Russia and Eastern Europe in general: blinis with crème fraîche and caviar, traditionally consumed on Orthodox Christmas Day (and afterwards). Our blini is green because of the plankton added by Andalusian chef Ángel León: it gives the dough a pronounced hint of seaweed/matcha tea. Green is also the colour of the tomatoes we use to make a sour butter that can be brushed on top of our soft plankton buns. There is caviar, but in this case, it's not made from roe – instead it's a 'mustard caviar' obtained by cooking mustard grains in a barbecued fish broth. This is how we pick out the complexity of the individual flavours: the sweetness of the blini, the acidity of the tomato butter and the toasted flavour of the fish.

Soft plankton buns and mustard caviar

SOFT SQUASH BUNS AND TROUT

With this further 'soft bites' option *(see also Soft plankton buns and mustard caviar on page 101)*, our gaze turns northwards to classic butter and salmon canapés. The bread component is a brioche bun, the flavour of which is enriched by the addition of squash and turmeric. The filling is a sweet-and-sour cream of carrot, squash and mushroom, slotted into the traditional V-shaped cut in the tops of the buns, in the manner of a 'maritozzo', a very popular Roman-style sweet leavened pastry. This little snack is topped by a fillet of marinated, smoked, thinly sliced trout, finished with a toasted pumpkin seed crumble, fragments of amaretti biscuits and salt.

BREAD, POLENTA AND BRUSCITT'

Bruscitt' is a dialect term for 'morsels' that comes from Busto Arsizio, in the suburbs between Milan and Varese. The morsels are actually unsold pieces of beef, pork and veal that were given away to the needy by butchers at the end of each day. Typically, these tasty leftovers were served up with generous portions of yellow polenta. Starting from this tradition, we have prepared a recipe with two key ingredients. Firstly, there is the sauce, made from pieces of vegetables lying around in the kitchen (shallots, carrots and celery), reduced and soaked in red wine and fennel. Secondly, there is the 'scarpetta', a soft white polenta flatbread, stuffed with braised beef, crying out to be dunked into the sauce. Beyond the religious and symbolic meanings of breaking and sharing bread, we think this dish is a very important one because it evokes confidence, familiarity, warmth and anticipation – all virtues that we celebrate at Cracco.

Bread, polenta and bruscitt'

LOVE IN PORTOFINO: BASIL PESTO, GREEN BEANS AND GRIDDLED POTATOES

This is a dish in which the caramelized Russian salad *(see page 61)* goes on holiday to Portofino, the delightful village in which our restaurant sits, in front of the Ligurian Sea. We gave our signature dish a local twist that could not be more typical of Portofino: in short, we added Liguria's most famous ingredient, traditional basil pesto, along with green beans, potatoes and even garden peas. All of these ingredients are wrapped up in a very thin wafer of griddled potato, creating something resembling a spring roll. We add to the roll a sprinkling of miso powder and a little pine nut paste, providing richer and more savoury notes. This is actually a vegetarian dish but the consumption has a decidedly carnivorous feel.

VEGETABLE SAUCE FOR DIPPING

This is another exploration of the *scarpetta*, the ritual of scooping a sauce with bread, that is almost at the anthropological core of our culinary identity. The black bread is grilled, while the sauce is a jus made from kitchen vegetable scraps: celeriac (celery root), tomatoes, potatoes and carrots, all of which are toasted, simmered, strained and blended with a black truffle and Marsala sauce. Cutlery is superfluous, and in fact, we provide neither knives nor forks for this course. Teasing out those tasty morsels with one's bare hands is an essential part of the enjoyment.

Aubergine carpaccio alla Norma

AUBERGINE CARPACCIO ALLA NORMA

Norma is a famous opera by the Catanian composer Vincenzo Bellini: as a result of this opera, for Sicilians, the name Norma has become synonymous with excellence, so that people say, 'She's a Norma!' in appreciation for a job well done. From this saying, it's a short step to the naming of the best-known starter (appetizer) in Sicilian cuisine: 'pasta alla Norma', made with aubergines (eggplants), tomato and ricotta cheese – the quintessential expression of the traditional flavours of Sicily and southern Italy. In our dish, based on this Sicilian classic, we cook a whole aubergine in mozzarella water to an almost plastic consistency, making an aubergine carpaccio. We then enrich the thin slices of carpaccio with a dressing made from so-called 'forgotten tomatoes', which have been left to sweat out all of their juices, then emulsified with oil. The savoury sauce is finally turbocharged with a cream made from mozzarella, smoked provola and grated pecorino. A familiar performance, elevated to a higher and more delicate plane.

AVOCADO, KIWI AND CORIANDER

Before the technicalities of this recipe, we would like to emphasize its fundamental nature. Avocado, kiwi and coriander (cilantro) are ingredients traditionally far removed from Italian agriculture and cuisine. In recent years, however, global warming is changing the nature of what we eat, making us much more familiar with raw materials that we have always considered distant and exotic. Italy has therefore become the largest kiwi producer in Europe, while avocado crops are spreading like wildfire in the south of the country, along with other tropical ingredients such as pineapple, mango, papaya and even coffee. In our kitchens, we always think that change is nothing to be afraid of; rather, we need to adapt and assimilate the ingredients as they travel. After all, there was a time, not too long ago, when tomatoes or potatoes did not exist in our cuisine, whereas today they are omnipresent in Italian cookbooks.

With this in mind, we made a Sicilian avocado purée (a kind of guacamole minus the lime and chilli) by mixing it with the two other key ingredients: diced fresh kiwi fruit from our Vistamare estate in Romagna and coriander stalks, roughly chopped like chives. On top of this we place a thin slice of tuna roe and a coriander jelly. These are the techniques and raw materials of a future that has already arrived.

Avocado, kiwi and coriander

SOLE ALLA CACCIATORA

What has always fascinated us about sole is its huge versatility, well-known now, and also celebrated in the past, in the classic Italian and French cookbooks, whether served with seaweed and white butter, incorporated into a panzanella salad or simply enclosed in a lettuce leaf and barbecued. In fact, sole can serve as a vehicle for many different combinations of ingredients, because it is a very delicate white meat with little hint of the sea, which is why we have always treated it as if it were almost more of a product of the land.

Our Sole alla cacciatora combines this deep-sea fish with a form of seasoning that is very popular in Italy, but more commonly used for chicken or rabbit: our cacciatora contains a little tomato, mushrooms, thyme and rosemary. We then create a mixed base with fish bones and chicken wings and add peppers, mushrooms and herbs. Finally, we roast the sole, enclose it in a crepinette (pork sausage parcel) and place it in the centre of the plate. The effect of the finished dish is as if we see a woodsman wading through the sea.

VICENZA-STYLE TROUT AND BITTER COCOA

Over the years, we have tried our hand several times at 'baccalà mantecato alla Vicentina', the signature dish of Carlo Cracco's hometown. To be precise, the main ingredient is not salted cod but 'stockfish' (air-dried cod). Traditionally, we wrap the stockfish in foil and boil it, then whip it up in a blender along with oil, salt, garlic, parsley and a little cream. For our dish, we use the same method on trout, a freshwater fish. Generally speaking, we increasingly prefer to cook river (or lake) fish for a number of reasons, but primarily because of the more delicate flavour of the flesh and the sustainability of the freshwater fish, which are wrongly regarded as lower in quality than their sea cousins. Our trout is served in a Vicenza-style sauce that is flavoured with cocoa, which we often use as a flavouring spice, like coffee.
This fascinating combination of tastes and textures – fishy, milky and bitter – is a blend that we've always enjoyed, and fortunately not just us.

Vicenza-style trout and bitter cocoa

VIGNAROLA OF HOME-GROWN VEGETABLES WITH CAPERS AND BRUSCANDOLI

Vignarola is a very popular recipe in the countryside of central Italy: its name is said to derive from the 'vignaroli', the vine cultivators who used to come home with a basket full of vegetables, uprooted from the gardens surrounding the vineyards. Vignarola is essentially a spring dish, which we've been cooking even more often since we took over the Vistamare farm in Santarcangelo di Romagna. This farm is spread over a hill covering about sixteen hectares, dotted with magnificent expressions of the countryside: vegetable gardens with both rare and common species, centuries-old olive trees producing a delicate extra-virgin oil, trees laden with peaches, cherries and apricots – and, of course, vineyards, from which we obtain a red Sangiovese and two white wines vinified in amphorae, using a blend of local grapes and a pure Trebbiano.

The components of our Vignarola romagnola depend on the weeks in which we harvest the vegetables: there may be artichokes, piattoni beans, asparagus, mangetout (snow peas), green peas and broad (fava) beans... We cook each vegetable separately, respecting its individual characteristics, but without browning them as tradition would dictate. We then cream them with a bitter butter of capers and bruscandoli – the shoots of the wild hop – and finish them off with roasted guanciale, jasmine flowers and pickled pea shoots. A different portrait of Romagna in the spring, every time we serve it.

WARM SPAGHETTI WITH A BARBECUED FISH, TOMATO AND GINGER SAUCE

This dish may not be as popular as the rice salad of our summers of yore, but pasta salad has always very much floated our boat, with popular but also 'refined' variations – just think of the reception given to Gualtiero Marchesi's cold spaghetti with caviar and chives.
Two main responses are evoked by this dish: the first sensation relates to the cool temperature of the pasta, and the second concerns the distinct personality of the grilled fish stew. The spaghetti is served lukewarm to ensure the overall freshness of the preparation, especially the deliberately raw tomato sauce and the spicy fresh ginger. The pasta itself is 'mantecata' (creamed) and bursting with the fragrance of the fish stew, which is the latest product of our long-term experimentation with broths, reductions and stocks.
The stew is dominated by an appetizing roasted note overall, and its rather pulpy texture adds backbone to the freshness of the pasta and the raw celery leaves, which ultimately round out the aromatic feel of the dish.

Lumachine alla Marinara with mussels and glasswort

LUMACHINE ALLA MARINARA WITH MUSSELS AND GLASSWORT

The main ingredients of this first course are deliberately not included in the name of the dish, because we prefer the diner to discover them purely by taste. We're talking about the red and black plums from our Romagna estate of Vistamare – here they stand in for the tomato, an interchangeability born of a surprisingly similar sourness and acidity. In this version of 'cozze alla marinara', the marinara comprises plums, garlic, parsley and anchovies. In our opinion, the 'lumachine' (snail-shaped) style of pasta is well suited to this sauce, and the glasswort adds a pleasant savouriness to the overall rounded acidity.

MIXED PASTA IN CHESTNUT AND MUSHROOM SOUP WITH RED WINE, BAY LEAF AND MASCARPONE

'Zuppa di funghi e castagne' (mushroom and chestnut soup) often turns up in Lombardian recipe books – it's a product of rustic expertise employing the two ingredients that truly symbolize our Italian autumn (fall). In the original recipes, fresh porcini mushrooms, chanterelles and chestnuts were cooked together in a broth seasoned with red wine, and this is essentially what we do, with the addition of some red port, reduced down to give extra strength. We stir several different types of pasta into this soup, copying the way that pasta and beans are traditionally blended in southern Italy. The final dish produces a highly concentrated and very rich spectrum of flavours, not least because of the addition of a fresh bay leaf extract. Our final touch is a spoonful of mascarpone, a little memory of the cheese rinds we used to dip into soups and minestrones at the end of the meal.

Mixed pasta in chestnut and mushroom soup, with red wine, bay leaf and mascarpone

BUCKWHEAT, APPLE AND PORK

Once again, the original spark for this dish was Lombardian peasant wisdom, bringing together pork rinds, Grana Padano rinds and parsley in a broth. This kind of soup was very popular in the countryside, providing the necessary energy to face the hard work in the fields, and eagerly anticipated as the overwhelming set of aromas reached the nose.
We cook the buckwheat in a broth of grilled ham, rather like a barley soup, then we stir in Castelmagno cheese, chives and a creamy apple sauce. The jelly we place on top of the soup is also made of toasted buckwheat. The diner lifts up the jelly to reveal the glorious fragrances of other times and places.

La Milano che avanza: marinated bread cutlet

LA MILANO CHE AVANZA: MARINATED BREAD CUTLET

This recipe evokes a tradition once common in our trattorias, whereby leftover Milanese-style veal chops were pickled for later consumption. In our case, the classic fried slice of veal itself has been replaced by a slice of leftover black bread, which is treated in exactly the same way as a schnitzel. We soak it in a reduced concentrate of roasted meat, dip it in flour and egg, fry it, then marinate it in a 'carpione' of wine, white vinegar, honey and other flavourings. It's basically a 'leftover bread cutlet', complete with all the feel of the old trattoria cutlets, sending the brain reeling with long-forgotten flavours, now revived and transformed by our new textures and tastes.

RABBIT À LA ROYALE BLANCHE

The original inspiration for this dish is 'lièvre à la royale', one of the legendary recipes of classical French cuisine, first properly summarized in 1755 by French writer Joseph Menon. Like the original French braised hare, our recipe is an excellent example of the rather untranslatable concept of cucina cucinata (literally 'cooked cooking'): a combination of complex processes, techniques and cooking styles involving a degree of time and effort that far surpasses the simple assembly of ingredients. Rather than hare, we use rabbit, which is a rather undervalued animal in today's kitchens. Rabbits produce a very delicate meat, which Italian chefs cook in the three ways that the gastronome Pellegrino Artusi recommended almost a century and a half ago: stewed, baked or roasted. Ours is a stuffed rabbit that includes mascarpone in the stuffing, a trick reminiscent of the use of curdled milk, which was once used to moisten meat that was too dry. The pale colour of the rabbit and the mascarapone is reiterated by other integral ingredients: the white rabbit stock, almond milk, white port and white pine nuts. The original Menon recipe used the hare's blood to bind the sauce together, but we use rabbit livers for this purpose. Finally, we add mastic tree oil, an arboreal fragrance that elevates the dish to extraordinary heights. This is the final stage of a process that is always important to us, and which many kitchens now neglect: the daily exercise of cooking the same things every day while always seeking to improve them. The endless repetition of a dish can only achieve great heights if the preparation is triggered by deep emotional involvement.

Rabbit à la royale blanche

Braised oxtail, cumin and cherries

BRAISED OXTAIL, CUMIN AND CHERRIES

A cultural barrier divides the northern Mediterrean from the south, and today, mainly for political and social reasons, there is much less exchange of ingredients and techniques between the two sides of Mare Nostrum than there was in the distant past. At Cracco's, we've always had a passionate interest in the cookbooks of North African or Middle Eastern traditions, and our oxtail dish bears brief testimony to this infatuation. Adapting the Persian custom of sealing meat in a soft dough with predominantly sweet notes, it includes a soft biscuit made of choux pastry, cocoa powder and whisked egg whites, all baked in a steam oven. The other key ingredient is oxtail sauce alla vaccinara, a popular Roman-style stew, here disguised in a Middle Eastern mask. Instead of raisins, we use coriander, cumin and cherries. Normally, on a menu, the bridging dish between savoury and sweet dishes is the 'pre-dessert', which is often a small dessert-like course. This dish, however, is a kind of small main course that actually anticipates the desserts at the end of the meal, an artifice that we love at Cracco's because we find it entirely consistent with the historical traditions of Lombardy cuisine.

TENDER BONE MARROW AND SMOKED ALMONDS

Veal marrow. Whether you eat it from the middle of the ossobuco, on the side or on top of saffron risotto, it's a central ingredient of Milanese cuisine. But it's also a star player in Cracco's cuisine, where we've enjoyed cooking it for more than two decades. In this dish, the role of the veal marrow is unusual in that, firstly, it is the dominant feature of the recipe (rather than simply being a garnish, as may often be the case), and secondly, it appears as the final stage of the savoury courses, serving as a prologue to dessert. The dish's concentrated gelatinous texture derives from several different constituents that quite unexpectedly complement one other – this is an alchemy reminiscent of the traditional Veronese pearà sauce, which normally accompanies boiled meat. There is the sweetness of the Parmiggiano, the silky smokiness of almond cream and the unsuspected balsamicity of boiled (not blanched) parsley. This is a veritable shot-gun marriage of ingredients that unexpectedly survives the honeymoon.

Tender bone marrow and smoked almonds

Pigeon and black pudding-stuffed cabbage

PIGEON AND BLACK PUDDING-STUFFED CABBAGE

This winter dish focuses on two key components. The first is 'sanguinaccio', the popular Italian blood sausage, which encases the pig's innards and blood using a recipe that is common in several countries of Europe, where it is variously known as black pudding, morcilla, boudin, blutwurst and finally 'marzapane' in Lombardy (not to be confused with the Apulian almond paste confection). The second element is pigeon, an ingredient heavy with symbolism, both now and in the past. Like the sanguinaccio, this bird has a strong blood component. For our dish, we bake a skinless pigeon breast and serve it with a black pudding stuffing and a 'brunoise' of sweet potato and corn sauce. The stuffed pigeon breast is wrapped first in a buckwheat crêpe brushed with mustard, and then wrapped again, this time in a blanched Savoy cabbage leaf. This elaborate dish expresses all our pleasure in the laborious preparations of the classical French cuisine, but the resulting tastes and textures are deeply Italian, particularly akin to the fascinating products of our countertop gastronomy. This recipe evokes a treasure trove of complex winter moods.

ROASTED BONE MARROW, SAFFRON AND GREMOLADA

Legend has it that, in 1574, Valerio di Fiandra, a Flemish artisan working on the stained-glass windows of Milan's Duomo, accidentally dropped saffron on the rice that had been prepared for his daughter's wedding. This chance event was allegedly the inspiration for a dish that has become the most popular first course in the Milanese tradition: 'yellow risotto'. Saffron and rice were eventually combined with veal marrow and gremolada, then seasoned with parsley, garlic and lemon zest, to create a more acidic and suave dish. These are the same ingredients that we have tried to blend in various ways in producing a tasty dish that is usually consumed in the 'final straight' of the meal, after the savoury dishes. We barbecue the marrow, combine it with a light saffron gel, then add the fragrance of garlic and the aromatic scent of parsley.
A yellow risotto, but with gremolada rather than rice.

Pear, gorgonzola dolce and mostarda

PEAR, GORGONZOLA DOLCE AND MOSTARDA

We are great supporters of the combination of cheese and pears. And this is certainly not our own personal discovery: in thirteenth-century France, the proverb 'God never made such a successful marriage as that between pears and cheese' was already in common parlance.
Let's also remember the saying in Italian courts: 'Don't let the farmer know how good cheese with pears is', they used to say. As if to imply: if this secret is revealed, the farmers will insist on keeping this delicious pairing for themselves rather than allowing it to be enjoyed exclusively at aristocratic tables. As ardent culinary democrats, we want to spread the message as far and wide as possible.
To make our case as strongly as possible, we make a pear sorbet – seasoned with oil, chives and mostarda (fruit in a mustard-infused syrup) – and place it in a small glass, dousing it with a whipped cream of gorgonzola. This is not a fusion, but a clear juxtaposition of dissimilar notes, generating an unremitting and exquisite interplay between sweet and salty. For us, this dish represents a new way of heralding the desserts to come – not through the usual serving of a sour sorbet 'to cleanse the palate', but with a complex aromatic savouriness intertwined with a slight spiciness. This recipe is simply a different take on another aspect of our traditional cuisine: the spoonful of jam with which we sweeten a slice of cheese.

STRAWBERRIES AND FRAGOLINO

Our chef Luca Sacchi has an inordinate passion for red fruits: when crates of raspberries or strawberries arrive from our Vistamare estate in Romagna, there is always the risk of them disappearing in his direction. If we're lucky, they may reappear in the form of a delicious dessert like this one. Here, strawberry pulp is combined with wild strawberries, red shiso leaves, strawberry and Angostura bitters sorbet (a dominant flavour), strawberry sugar and, finally, our own Fragolino sparkling wine. The result is a vivid red dish that focuses on the creaminess and voluptuousness that all of our favourite desserts possess in spades.

Strawberries and Fragolino

RICE PUDDING ARANCINI

Here's a dessert with a thousand stories to tell. The first and most important one comes from the combination of rice and milk, which takes us back to childhood, when for snacks our grandparents used to prepare this kind of milk soup, mixing it with a few fistfuls of rice and a spoonful of sugar. We started with this nostalgic vision, dressing it up in an even more special outfit, suitable perhaps for Christmas festivities. We create a kind of arancino, consisting of a creamy layer of rice and milk and a core of mascarpone and zabaglione, covered with sea salt. At the dining table, we serve it with a stylized snowflake, made with lemon syrup, and a cup that releases aromas and scents of citrus, cinnamon, cloves, vanilla and ginger. These are the familiar scents of the Christmas hearth, elevated from their original rustic form to create more profound rituals and gastronomic meanings.

Burnt chocolate and blanched parsley

BURNT CHOCOLATE AND BLANCHED PARSLEY

Dessert is always a crucial stage of the meal for us. In contrast to the classic cuisine, we believe it is important to serve desserts that have some continuity with the preceding dishes. This is why we often introduce important savoury or vegetable notes in the traditionally sweet part of the menu, while trying not to underplay the voluptuous nature of the dessert. This dish consists of a classic Bavarian component in the form of a small toasted white chocolate log, combined with parsley sauce, sorbet and a blanched-parsley salad. These abundant herbal and balsamic notes are then counterpointed and enhanced with salted almonds and the hybrid sweetness of salted caramel. Sweet, vegetal, savoury. Savoury, vegetal, sweet.

FROZEN FRUIT ASSORTMENT

We have always loved sorbets at the end of a meal. However, we wanted something that went beyond serving the classic two balls of sorbet, presented in the traditional fashion in a bowl. We have therefore taken a more playful approach, seeking first and foremost to create a feast for the eye, while trying to retain the two core values of the dish: freshness and taste. We patiently reproduce in silicone moulds the iced shapes of three fruit slices: watermelon, passion fruit and coconut. At least this is what we call them, though their contents are something slightly different: the watermelon slice is actually a green apple jelly with white chocolate, raspberry sorbet and basil seeds. The passion fruit slice is a blueberry jelly with fior di latte and mango jelly, topped with passion fruit. Finally, the coconut slice is a chocolate jelly with cocoa nibs and coconut milk. Playful but also deadly serious – because it's very important for our diners to be able to appreciate the colours and natural sweetness.

Frozen fruit assortment

CHOCOLATE AND LARDO SOUFFLÉS

We have boundless esteem for all those artisans who have instigated crucial departures from standard historical styles of cooking. One of these is certainly Pierre Hermé, a true professional from Alsace who steered the destiny of pastry making in a different direction. Today we take it for granted that dark chocolate and salt co-exist in many recipes, but we owe this key development to Hermé, a pastry chef who was totally dedicated to his profession, always cooking tasty dishes using only natural ingredients and never resorting to anything artificial.

Gold bars and silver nuggets

GOLD BARS AND SILVER NUGGETS

Italy has a long tradition of biscotti (literally 'twice-baked'), stretching back for almost a thousand years. Historians agree that the use of sugar only became widespread in Europe after the twelfth century, at the time of the Crusades, when it also began to be used in cooking as an essential complement to butter.
We wanted to embellish this long history in two ways: firstly, by making our biscuits ingot-shaped, and secondly by colouring them gold and silver. Our gold ingot, incorporating chocolate, salt and coffee, has the very fine texture of a classic biscuit (cookie) while also being extremely rich in butter and chocolate. The silver ingot, which includes white chocolate and muscovado, is the result of a laborious process that colours the classic nugget white – this biscuit has hints of liquorice and a very pronounced sweetness and fatness.

DARK CHOCOLATE AND DRIED OLIVES

A minimalist version of an important traditional Italian dessert: Cremino with chocolate, olives and fior di latte with capers. Ours uses true Cremino, producing a rectangular dark chocolate ganache enhanced by a Taggiasca olive infusion and finished with caper milk for a highly distinct fragrance. Once again, the interplay between chocolate and salt is important here, offering a contrast that we know is addictive.

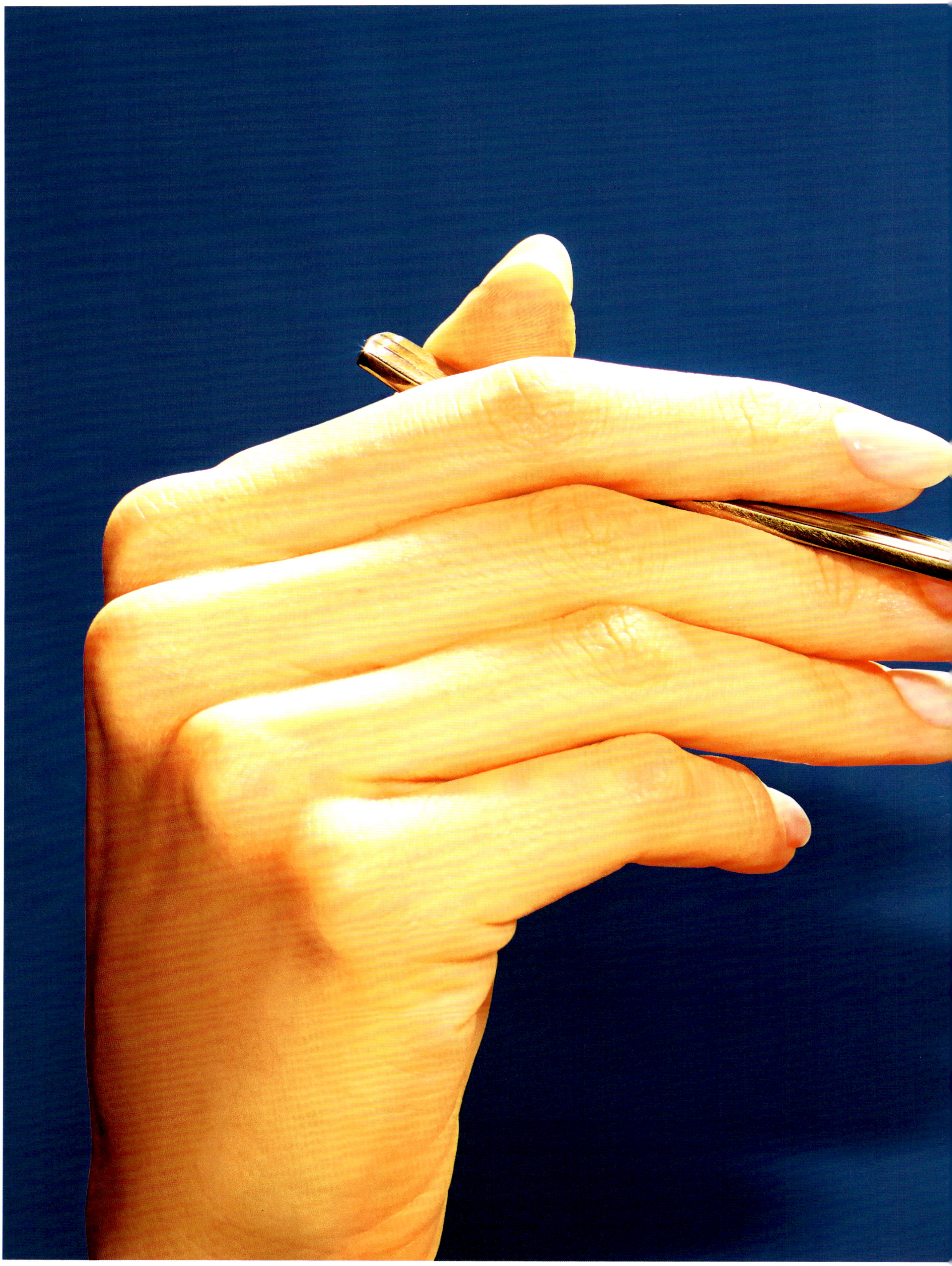

Dark chocolate and dried olives

BARBAJADA

Barbajada is a drink that was popular in Milan from the late eighteenth to the early twentieth century. It owes its name to Domenico Barbaja, a citizen who totally embodied the city's motto of 'Milan with heart in hand' (an expression of the Milanese desire to do their bit for others). Despite Barbaja being celebrated in later life as the director of such venerable institutions as the Teatro alla Scala, he has actually been down in history for a quite different reason, which relates to the time, much earlier in his career, when he was working as an apprentice at the Caffè dei Virtuosi in Via Manzoni, always frequented by intellectuals, musicians and visitors. Barbaja came up with the idea of serving chocolate, milk and coffee in equal parts, then frothing them up with a whisk. This recipe was successful right from the start, not least because it was suitable for all seasons: in winter it could be served hot with cream in a cup; and in summer it was drunk cool in a glass. At Cracco's, we prepare our barbajadas in a distinctly austere, cold version, topping it with whipped milk foam and 'grue de cacao' (crunchy pieces of roasted cacao beans). Customers really appreciate this as they did in the past.

1
4
5
8
12
11
15

2
3
7
6
9
10
13
14
17
18
16

COOKWARE

Small risotto pan or milk-frothing jug 1

For cooking two or three servings of risotto-style rice.

Round roasting tin (pan) 2

For cooking small joints of meat or poultry.

Pans of different diameters 3; 7; 9; 11

For slow and prolonged cooking or for browning or deep-frying, ensuring that ingredients do not overlap.

Sauté pans 4; 12

For quickly sautéing vegetables or searing small cuts of meat and fish.

Roasting tin (pan) 5

For roasting poultry and joints of meat, and for roasted vegetable dishes. Those with medium-high sides that leave enough room for browning are the best.

Saucepan 6

To reheat or finish preparing ready-made meat and fish stocks or finished sauces that need to be brought to the appropriate temperature and possibly enhanced with a flavouring ingredient.

Steel pan 8

For boiling meat or vegetables or cooking pasta or rice. A basic, high-sided pan that is indispensable, thanks to its sturdiness and superior heat conductivity.

Copper serving pan 10

Used to bring dishes served by the waiter into the dining room. Shiny and aesthetically striking, it serves as the final container for dishes such as some short pastas, risottos, garnishes or small vegetables.

Braising pans 13; 16

For cooking over a flame or griddle before being placed in the oven.

Copper bastardella (hemispherical) pan 14

Traditionally used to make zabaglione and some mother sauces in classic cuisine. Until very recently, a paste made of vinegar, flour and coarse salt would be used to polish its copper surfaces and make it look like new. It then had to be rinsed and dried carefully to prevent oxidation starting again.

Conical sieve (strainer), or chinois 15

For straining stocks and broths. To clarify these liquids even further, strain through a fine-mesh conical sieve.

Stainless-steel cloche 17

Mainly used for table service to add a touch of elegance and importance to dishes served in the dining room.

Traditional fish kettle 18

For preparing court-bouillons in which to poach whole fish. The fish is placed on a rack which is lowered into the pan. The removable rack allows the fish to be taken out whole after cooking.

KNIVES

From left to right

MEAT KNIVES

Fine boning knife

A very sharp and thin but robust blade used for boning small cuts of meat without spoiling the delicate flesh of rabbits, or the meat of chickens and other birds.

Gyuto

Comparable to the classic Western chef's knife, it has a rigid and firm blade suitable for cutting large quantities of vegetables or meat.

Yanagiba

A sturdy and rigid knife designed to cleanly and precisely slice portioned cuts of meat.

Garawuki (in the foreground)

A boning knife with a large handle which enables the user to apply the force needed to bone very tough cuts of meat. This Japanese-style knife is made by an artisan from Valdobbiadene, Treviso.

Large boning knife (in the foreground)

Designed to slide over the bones of large animals, such as veal, cows or pigs, peeling off the meat without damaging it. The thick and rigid blade is not intended for slicing, so the proper way to use it is to always work from the tip.

VEGETABLE AND FISH KNIVES

Paring knife

A small and light knife with a very rigid and sturdy spine, ideal for cutting vegetables into small pieces and for fine detailing.

Filleting knife

Despite its good flexibility, this knife has a long and tough blade for guiding along the backbone of the fish, fully removing the fillet without leaving any flesh attached.

Sujihiki

This filleting knife has a rigid blade that is also suitable for slicing meat across the grain. The grooves beaten into the steel keep meat from sticking to the blade, preventing it from being damaged or broken.

Unagi-saki

Specially designed for cleaning and filleting eels, this knife has a special shape that allows it to remove the maximum amount of meat by sliding over the backbone, leaving the valuable and delicate meat intact.

Deba

Featuring a very strong blade, this knife is suitable for slicing the meat and bones of large fish and birds. Being heavy, it makes for clean and safe chopping.

Mini-cleaver

Forged by European craftsmen in the Japanese style, this knife allows you to cut large amounts of short vegetables and medium meat cuts.

LAGUIOLE

出刃包丁

RECIPES

FROM THE RESTAURANT

Amuse-bouche in The Fumoir

Caramelized Russian salad

Serves 15

FOR THE MAYONNAISE

160 g	**potatoes**, peeled and cut into 5-mm/¼-inch uniform dice
110 g	**carrots**, cut into 5-mm/¼-inch uniform dice
20 g	**egg**
3 g	**salt**
2 ml	**lemon juice**
2 ml	**white wine vinegar**
290 g	**sunflower oil**
20 g	**peas**, blanched
10 g	**capers,** desalted
40 g	**tuna in oil**, drained

Cook the potatoes and carrots separately in a pan of plenty of salted water until tender (they should remain firm to the bite without crumbling). Drain and place in a large bowl of iced water, then pat dry with kitchen paper (paper towels). Make a classic mayonnaise by blending the egg, 3 g salt, lemon juice, vinegar and oil. Mix the potatoes, carrots, peas, capers and tuna in a large container and stir in the mayonnaise until well coated and evenly distributed.

FOR THE CAPER SUGAR

300 g	**fondant icing**
100 g	**glucose syrup**
100 g	**isomalt granules**
8 g	**capers**, desalted and dried
1,5 g	**Maldon sea salt**

Combine the fondant icing, glucose and isomalt in a large pan and cook until it reaches 160°C/320°F on a sugar (candy) thermometer. Remove from the heat and add the capers and salt. Pour the mixture onto a sheet of baking parchment and spread it out as much as possible to allow it to quickly crystallize. When the sheet has cooled, break it into pieces and grind in a blender to make the caper sugar. Using a sieve (strainer), sprinkle a layer of caper sugar over a stencil mat with 7.5-cm-/3-inch-diameter cavities. Lift off the stencil and use a kitchen blowtorch to melt the sugar. Allow the sugar discs to cool and then store them in a container with silica gel packets in a cool, dry place.

ASSEMBLY

Spread a scant tablespoon of Russian salad on a sugar disc and flatten slightly. Cover with another sugar disc and press down gently. Using the blowtorch, heat the edges to melt and seal the filling inside. Turn over and repeat heating the edges to finish sealing and obtain a crisp sugar shell filled with the salad. Serve immediately.

Tongue terrine in a brioche crust

Serves 8

FOR THE BRIOCHE DOUGH

25 ml	**warm milk**
5 g	**fresh yeast**
25 g	**caster (superfine) sugar**
200 g	**strong white flour** (W index 280–350), plus extra for dusting
15 g	**acacia honey**
100 g	**egg**
60 g	**unsalted butter**, cut into small pieces
4 g	**salt**
	oil, for greasing
50 g	**liquid sourdough starter**

Pour the warm milk into a bowl, stir in the yeast together with a teaspoon of the sugar and leave to rest for 10 minutes, or until you get a light foam. In a large bowl or in a stand mixer, combine the flour, the remaining sugar, the honey and eggs. Add the milk mixture and start kneading with the dough hook or by hand until it forms a homogenous dough. Continue to work the dough for at least 8–10 minutes to develop the gluten, then add the butter, one piece at a time, waiting for each portion to be completely incorporated before adding the next. Then add the salt and continue working until the dough is smooth, shiny and elastic. Transfer the dough to a lightly oiled bowl, cover with cling film (plastic wrap) or a kitchen cloth and allow to rise at room temperature until it doubles in volume, 2–3 hours. Turn the risen dough out onto a lightly floured surface, gently deflate it and form it, as you prefer: for example, by plaiting (braiding), or dividing it into balls and placing them in a buttered mould. Cover again and allow to prove for a further 1–2 hours until the dough reaches the edge of the mould.

FOR THE CHICKEN MOUSSELINE

110 g	**fresh chicken breast and wing meat**
75 g	**béchamel sauce** (made with 180 g roux per litre of milk)
1	**tablespoon grated Parmigiano Reggiano cheese**
66 g	**egg yolk**
	salt and ground black pepper
	grated nutmeg, as needed

Pass the chicken meat through a mincer (grinder) twice, keeping it well chilled. Mix with the remaining ingredients and season with salt, pepper and grated nutmeg. Set aside.

FOR THE PEAR AND MUSTARD CREAM

100 g **Abate pear**
2 g **Worcestershire sauce**
50 g **red shallot vinegar**
1 g **salt**
ground white pepper
0.2 g **xanthan gum**
10 g **wholegrain mustard**

FOR THE VEAL TONGUE TERRINE

30 g **boiled veal tongue**, cut into 2-mm-/1⁄16-inch-thick slices
50 g **mixture of egg yolk** (45%), **mustard** (45%) **and cornflour (cornstarch)** (10%)
50 g **aged lardo (cured pork back fat)**, thinly sliced
30 g **black truffle**, sliced
70 g **Abate pear** (not overly ripe), cut into slices the same size as the tongue
300 g **Swiss chard leaves**, blanched and refreshed in iced water
250 g **chicken mousseline**
300 g **brioche dough**
1 **egg yolk**, for brushing
Maldon sea salt

Vacuum-seal the pear in a vacuum bag and cook sous-vide for 30 minutes at 85°C/185°F. Allow to cool, then blend with the remaining ingredients, except the mustard, and season with pepper to taste. Transfer the mixture to a container and incorporate the mustard. Set aside.

To make the terrine, arrange three layers of tongue slices brushed with the egg and mustard mixture inside a terrine mould and top with a layer of lardo slices, another of truffle slices and another of pear slices. Repeat the process, then cover with three more layers of tongue. Unmould the terrine, wrap in the blanched chard leaves and spread with the chicken mousseline. Place the filling in the centre of the rolled-out brioche dough. Wrap the terrine in the brioche dough to form a smooth and compact envelope. Prove at room temperature for 30 minutes, then brush with egg yolk and season with Maldon salt. Preheat the oven to 160°C/325°F and bake for 13 minutes. Once cooked, allow to cool and slice as required. Serve with the pear and mustard cream.

Nori, veal tongue and date

Serves 10

FOR THE NORI PUFFS

100 g **cooked buckwheat**
150 g **White rice base** (see page 196)
1.5 g **salt**
8 **nori squares** (standard size)
oil, for deep-frying

Mix the cooked buckwheat with the rice base and salt until combined. Spread 30 g of the mixture on each nori square and dry out in the oven. Deep-fry in hot oil until puffed, then drain on kitchen paper (paper towels).

FOR THE PICKLED DATE PURÉE

125 ml **white wine**
90 g **Tropea red onion**
75 ml **apple cider vinegar**
50 ml **white vinegar**
25 g **acacia honey**
10 ml **red shallot vinegar**
5 g **ground white pepper**
1 **bay leaf**
1 **sage leaf**
200 ml **water**
150 g **pitted Californian dates**

Make a pickling liquor by boiling all the ingredients, excepting the dates, with the water, then strain. Allow the pickling liquor to cool, then vacuum-seal together with the dates and pickle for at least a month in the fridge. Drain the pickled dates and blend to a smooth purée.

FOR THE VEAL TONGUE

120 g **veal tongue**, boiled and thinly sliced
extra-virgin olive oil, for seasoning
8 g **white sesame paste**
20 g **pickled date** pureé
20 g **candied chinotto in mustard-flavoured syrup**
ground white pepper

ASSEMBLY

When it is time to serve, season the tongue with olive oil and salt. Coat the nori puffs with sesame paste, arrange the cooked veal tongue on top and season with the pickled date purée. Garnish with strips of candied chinotto and season with white pepper.

Soft saffron buns, gold and caviar

Serves 10

FOR THE SAFFRON HONEY

0.2 g **saffron threads**
300 g **acacia honey**

Add the saffron and honey to an airtight jar, seal with a lid and allow to infuse in a cool, dark place for 30 days

FOR THE SOFT SAFFRON BUNS

40 g **fresh yeast**
85 ml **milk**
250 g **soft wheat flour** (W index 180–230)
0.5 g **liquorice root powder**
0.5 g **saffron powder**
50 g **eggs**, beaten (for the dough)
25 g **caster (superfine) sugar**
5 g **salt**
50 g **unsalted butter**, cut into small pieces, softened
30 g **eggs** (for glazing)
5 ml **double (heavy) cream**

In a bowl, dissolve 20 g of the yeast in room temperature milk. Combine the flour, liquorice root powder and saffron powder in a stand mixer fitted with a dough hook and while mixing, add the milk and yeast mixture. As soon as a dough forms, mix in the beaten eggs, a third at a time, then add the sugar and salt and mix until the dough is smooth. Continue mixing, incorporating the softened butter in small pieces. Cover the dough and allow to rest in the fridge overnight.

The next day, gently knead the dough by stretching and folding it, taking care not to allow it to develop structure. Divide the dough into 22-g portions and shape each portion into balls by rotating and compacting them. Place the dough balls on perforated baking trays. Mix the remaining 30 g egg and cream together in a bowl, then brush the dough balls with some of the egg wash. Allow to rise until doubled in size in a warm spot. Preheat a steam oven to 110°C/230°F (or place a roasting tin/pan filled with water on the bottom of a regular oven to create steam). Brush the doughballs with more egg wash and bake for 14 minutes. Allow to cool with the baking trays placed on top of the buns to keep the tops flat.

FOR THE SAFFRON PASTRY CREAM

500 ml **milk latte fresco intero**
0.25 g **saffron powder**
0.1 g **saffron threads**
30 g **shallot**
2 g **salt**
80 g **caster (superfine) sugar**
66 g **egg yolk**
60 g **soft wheat flour** (W index 180–230)

In a pan, combine the milk with the saffron, shallot and salt and heat to 90°C/194°F. Turn off the heat, cover the pan with cling film (plastic wrap) and allow to steep for 10 minutes. Strain, then use the saffron-infused milk to make a pastry cream with the remaining ingredients. Cool quickly, vacuum-seal in a bag and set aside.

FOR THE SHALLOT GEL
500 g **shallots**
extra-virgin olive oil, for cooking
1 **bay leaf**
50 ml **white wine**
125 ml **red shallot vinegar**
15 g **acacia honey**
agar agar, as needed
salt

In a pan, sauté the shallots in olive oil with the bay leaf. Season with salt. Add the white wine and vinegar, then add enough water to cover. Add the honey and cook until the shallot layers are completely cooked through. Remove and discard the bay leaf, then purée the shallot mixture in a blender and strain through a sieve (strainer) into a bowl. Add 1 g agar-agar for every 100 g of purée obtained and allow to cool and set. Once set, blend to a smooth gel.

TO ASSEMBLE
10 **soft saffron buns** (see above)
120 g **saffron pastry cream** (see above)
30 g **shallot gel** (see above)
30 g **caviar butter**
50 g **Amur Kaluga caviar**
10 g **saffron honey** (see above)
10 **edible gold leaf sheets**
Maldon sea salt

Warm the buns in a steam oven for less than 1 minute. Make a cavity in the top of each bun and fill with a nut-sized portion of saffron pastry cream. Using a syringe, pipe a drop of shallot gel and add two smears of caviar butter. Cover with a teaspoon of caviar. Brush the top of the saffron bun with saffron honey and season with salt flakes. Cover with gold leaf and serve.

Crispy rice crackers

Serves 4

FOR THE WHITE RICE BASE
250 g **Arborio rice**
7 g **salt**
750 ml **water**
oil, for deep frying

Combine the rice and salt in a large pan with the water. Bring to the boil and cook for 30–35 minutes until the rice is mushy and the liquid is absorbed. Transfer to a blender and blend to a smooth, sticky paste. Place a 250–300-g portion of the paste between two sheets of baking parchment and, using a small rolling pin, roll it out to form a 3–4-mm-/1/6-inch-thick sheet. Dry out in an oven preheated to 50°C/122°F with the vent open for 6 hours, or until completely dry. The result will be a crisp and translucent sheet. When ready to use, heat enough oil for deep-frying in a large, deep saucepan to 180°C/350°F, or until a cube of bread browns in 30 seconds. Carefully add a portion of the dried rice to the hot oil and deep-fry for a few seconds until puffed. Shake well to drain, using care as the hot oil may splatter, and immediately pat dry with kitchen paper (paper towels).

FOR THE BLACK RICE BASE
75 g **Arborio rice**
8 g **salt**, plus extra for salting the water
750 ml **water**
250 g **Venere black rice**

Cook the Arborio rice in a pan of boiling salted water and set aside. In a large pan, combine the water, the black rice and the 8 g salt. Bring to the boil and cook until the water is absorbed. When the liquid is completely absorbed, add the already cooked Arborio rice and blend to a smooth paste. Proceed in the same way as for the white rice base.

CRISPY RICE CRACKER VARIATIONS:

Rustic rice crackers
65 g **buckwheat flour**
65 g **maize flour**
500 ml **water**
2.5 g **salt**
100 g **white rice** base (see above)
oil, for deep-frying

Prepare a polenta with these ingredients and allow to cool, then mix it with the white rice base. Follow the directions for the white rice base to roll into sheets, dry and deep-fry until puffed.

Mediterranean tomato rice crackers
200 g **white rice** base
40 g **tomato purée (paste)**
4 g **colatura di alici (anchovy extract)**
1 g **dried oregano**
oil, for deep-frying

Blend the ingredients, then roll out into sheets 60 x 40 cm/24 x 16 inches and dry. Deep-fry in oil at a lower temperature oil to preserve the bright colour.

Saffron rice crackers
125 g **Arborio rice**
500 ml **water**
4 g **salt**
0.5 g **saffron powder**
oil, for deep-frying

Blend the ingredients, then roll out into sheets and dry. Deep-fry in oil at a lower temperature oil to preserve the bright colour.

Cuttlefish ink rice crackers
125 g **Arborio rice**
500 ml **water**
4 g **salt**
6 g **cuttlefish ink**
oil, for deep-frying

Follow the directions for the white rice base, adding the squid ink to the rice paste when blending. Roll into sheets, dry and deep-fry as directed.

Beetroot rice crackers
65 g **cooked beetroot (beet)**
500 ml **water**
125 g **Arborio rice**
4 g **salt**
oil, for deep-frying

Follow the directions for the white rice base and blend the cooked beetroot to obtain a brightly coloured and uniform mixture. Do not cook the beetroot with the rice, otherwise the colour will be brown and unappealing. Then, proceed as for the other types. Add the beetroot to the rice paste and blend together. Deep-fry in oil at a lower temperature oil to preserve the bright colour.

Mushroom rice crackers
125 g **Arborio rice**
500 ml **water**
4 g **salt**
5 g **dried porcini mushrooms**
2 g **soy sauce**
oil, for deep-frying

Follow the directions for the white rice base, cooking all the ingredients together and proceeding with rolling, drying and deep-frying.

At the table

Marinated egg yolk

FOR THE MARINATED EGG YOLK
45 g **caster (superfine) sugar**
125 g **smoked coarse salt**
30 g **plain bean purée**
(beans boiled and blended on their own)
25 ml **water**
10 **eggs**
extra-virgin olive oil, for brushing

Mix the sugar, salt, bean purée and the water together in a large bowl with a spoon. Spread a tablespoon of the marinade inside single-portion moulds. Separate the eggs and place a yolk in the centre of each mould, then cover with another tablespoon of the marinade. Take care not to break the yolk at any time. Store in a cool, dark, dry place for 3 hours. Use a spoon to turn the yolks over and allow to marinate for a further 3 hours. After marinating, lift the yolks out of the moulds and rinse them gently under cold running water. Pat dry with kitchen paper (paper towels). Brush with olive oil before serving.

FOR THE MARINATED EGG BUTTER
200 g **unsalted butter, softened**
200 g **marinated egg yolk** (see above), pressed through a fine-mesh sieve (strainer)

Once the butter is soft enough to work and the creamy marinated egg paste is at room temperature, add both ingredients to a mixer and mix until smooth. Mould into the desired shape or set aside in a piping (pastry) bag when ready to serve (preferably with Black bread; see page 272).

Tomato, mozzarella and basil

Serves 8

FOR THE TOMATO GEL
1 kg **Piccadilly tomatoes**, peeled and quartered
20 ml **water**
10 g **salt**
isinglass, as needed

In a blender, purée the tomatoes with the water and salt. Strain the purée and weigh the resulting juice. Pour the juice into a container. Weigh out 4.5 g of isinglass for every 100 g of tomato juice. Soak the isinglass in a bowl of cold water to rehydrate. In a pan, heat a tablespoon of the tomato juice to just over 40°C/104°F, add the isinglass and let it dissolve. Add the mixture to the remaining juice in the container, set over a bowl of iced water and allow to cool while stirring frequently until completely set. Transfer to a piping (pastry) bag and store in the fridge.

FOR THE MOZZARELLA FOAM
1 **isinglass** sheet
250 g **buffalo mozzarella cheese**
100 ml **fresh milk**
4 g **salt**

Soak the isinglass sheet in a bowl of cold water to rehydrate. In a Thermomix, combine the mozzarella, milk and salt and blend while heating to 55°C/131°F. Add the isinglass, blend for a few more seconds, then strain the mixture. Transfer to a 1-litre siphon and insert a nitrogen cartridge.

FOR THE BASIL OIL
500 g **basil leaves**, blanched for 3 minutes
50 g **fresh basil leaves**
700 g **extra-virgin olive oil**

Blend all the ingredients for 2 minutes, then strain the mixture through kitchen paper (paper towels) without pressing, collecting the clear and bright oil in a container.

FOR THE PLANKTON WAFER
5 g **freeze-dried plankton**
100 g **egg whites**
100 g **soft wheat flour** (W index 180–230)
100 g **unsalted butter**

Preheat the oven to 160°C/325°F. Dissolve the plankton in the egg whites, then make a batter with the ingredients, as if making lingue di gatto biscuits. Using a baking stencil, pipe the batter into desired shapes and bake for 9 minutes. Allow to cool, then store in a dry place.

FOR THE OLIVE, CAPERS AND SALTED ANCHOVY TARTARE
10 g **capers**, desalted
15 g **Raggia olives in oil**
5 g **salted anchovy fillets**

Finely chop all the ingredients with a knife and mix them together.

ASSEMBLY
Put ½ teaspoon of basil oil in the middle of a chosen serving plate or dish. Arrange a nut-sized serving of the olive, capers and anchovy tartare in the centre. Add ½ teaspoon of toasted breadcrumbs and dress with extra-virgin olive oil. Pipe some tomato gel onto each, then add some mozzarella foam on the top to cover and finish with a drizzle of oil, basil shoots, a pinch of dried anchovy powder and the plankton wafer.

Everyday salad

Makes 25 spheres

FOR THE BONITO BALLS
125 g **cooked bonito fillet**
18 g **radishes**, finely diced
1.5 g **chopped parsley**
1.5 g **fresh wasabi**
½ **teaspoon extra-virgin olive oil**
salt and ground white pepper

Crumble the cooked bonito into a large bowl and add the remaining ingredients. Mix well until combined. Use a mixer if necessary, taking care not to allow the mixture to heat. Season with salt and pepper. Shape 12–15-g portions of the mixture into small balls and freeze at -18°C/-0.4°F.

FOR THE RADISH GLAZE JELLY
250 g **radishes**, peeled (greens and root set aside for assembly later)
165 g **beetroot (beet)**, peeled
165 ml **water**
8 ml **white wine vinegar**
1.5 g **salt**
kappa carrageenan, as needed

Combine the radishes, beetroot (beet), water, vinegar and salt in a vacuum bag and seal at 100% vacuum. Cook sous-vide in a steam oven at 95°C/203°F for 1 hour 15 minutes, then blend until smooth and creamy. Weigh the cream and put it into a pan. Weigh out 1 g of kappa carrageenan per 100 g of cream, add it to the pan and bring to the boil. Remove the pan from the heat and dip the frozen bonito balls into the mixture to form a thin pink coating to give them the appearance of real radishes. If necessary, dip the balls a second time to form a slightly thicker coating. Set aside in the fridge.

FOR THE WHITE RADISH CREAM

375 g	**radishes**, red parts removed
75 g	**white turnip**
15 ml	**white wine vinegar**
0.5 g	**salt**

Combine all the ingredients in a vacuum bag and seal at 100% vacuum. Cook sous-vide in a steam oven at 95°C/203°F for 1 hour 15 minutes, then blend until smooth and creamy.

FOR THE LETTUCE CREAM

2	**heads cos lettuce**
	extra-virgin olive oil, for drizzling and cooking
1	**shallot**, finely chopped
20 g	**Taggiasche olives**
100 g	**spinach leaves**
	salt and ground black pepper

Wash the lettuce heads well, then secure them by tying them in two places with kitchen string (twine). Drizzle them with olive oil and place on a hot griddle just long enough to sear gently, barely wilting the leaves. Remove from the griddle and cut the lettuces into pieces. In a large pan, sauté the finely chopped shallot in olive oil until coloured, then add the olives and the seared lettuce pieces and cook the lettuce gently until soft. Remove from the heat and purée together with the spinach leaves in a blender until smooth and creamy. Season with salt and pepper.

ASSEMBLY

	caviar butter, as needed
	fresh caviar, as needed

Put a tablespoon of white radish cream in the middle of a serving plate. Add a smear of caviar butter, then place a bonito radish on top. Finish re-creating the radish by attaching the greens and root. Add a few drops of lettuce cream to the plate and finish with a teaspoon of fresh caviar.

Sea Salad World Tour

Serves 6

6	**scallop wafers** (see below)
6	**prawn (shrimp) wafers** (see below)
6	**cuttlefish wafers** (see below)
180 g	**snapper fillets**, cut into 1–2-cm/½–¾-inch cubes
40 ml	**citronette made with yuzu juice** (25 g extra virgin olive oil, 15 ml yuzu juice)
60 g	**herb jelly** (see below)
6	**mustard leaves**
6	**shiso purple cress**
6	**chamomile leaves**
6	**thin red chilli rings**
6	**shavings of tuna bottarga**
6	**thin fresh shallot rings**
2 g	**beetroot (beet) powder**
60	**freeze-dried sweetcorn kernels**
	extra-virgin olive oil
	sea salt flakes

FOR THE SEAFOOD WAFERS

Scallop: Blend 100 g of scallops, coral removed, to a smooth paste with 1/2 teaspoon of oil. Season with a pinch of salt.

Prawn: Blend 100 g of Sicilian red prawns (shrimp) to a paste similar to the scallop paste. Roll out the three seafood pastes separately between two sheets of baking parchment, 30 × 40 cm/12 × 16 inches in size, spreading it out thinly and evenly to make three sheets. Bake at 45°C/113°F for 40 minutes. Cool quickly, then cut into 4.5-cm/1¾-inch squares and store at -18°C/-0.4°F.

Cuttlefish: Blend 90 g of scallops, coral removed, with 10 g of fresh squid ink to a paste the same consistency as the previous two pastes.

FOR THE HERB JELLY

3 g	**isinglass sheets**
20 g	**fresh ginger**, peeled
8 g	**acacia honey**
200 ml	**water**
1 g	**chamomile leaves**
1 g	**lemon balm**
1	**geranium leaf**
1	**cinnamon leaf**
1 g	**mint**
0.7 g	**salt**
0.5 g	**timut pepper**
0.6 g	**agar-agar**

Soak the isinglass in a bowl of cold water to rehydrate. Bring the ginger, honey and the 200 ml water to the boil in a large pan, then turn off the heat. Add the herbs, cover with cling film (plastic wrap) and allow to steep for 4 minutes. Strain the liquid into a clean pan, add the salt, pepper and agar-agar and bring it back to the boil to dissolve the agar-agar. Add the rehydrated isinglass and allow to set in the fridge. Break up the jelly with a spoon before use

ASSEMBLY

Season the raw snapper cubes with the citronette and salt and divide them between six serving dishes. Slightly flatten the top of the fish cubes, then add 1/2 tablespoon of herb jelly, broken up with the spoon to each. Arrange a seafood wafer of each type in a decorative pile. Garnish with fresh herbs, a chilli and a shallot ring and bottarga. Lightly dust with beetroot (beet) powder and finish with freeze-dried sweetcorn kernels and a drizzle of extra-virgin olive oil.

Cannellini beans, sea urchins and tarragon

Serves 6

80 g	**sea urchin emulsion** (see below)
12	**fresh sea urchins**
60 g	**braised beans** (see below)
250 g	**cannellini bean foam** (see below)
25 g	**tarragon oil** (see below)
25	**wood sorrel leaves**
6	**crispy potato wafers**
8	**oyster leaves**, sliced into julienne strips
	Maldon sea salt

FOR THE SEA URCHIN EMULSION

75 g	**pasteurized egg yolk**
45 g	**white miso paste**
100 g	**sea urchin tongues**
0.5 g	**salt**
200 g	**clarified butter**, melted
	freshly ground white pepper

In a mixing beaker, blend the egg yolk, miso paste and sea urchin tongues with a hand-held blender. Add the salt, then whisk in the melted clarified butter a little at a time to an emulsion. Season with pepper.

FOR THE CANNELLINI BEAN FOAM

1	**tablespoon extra-virgin olive oil**
100 g	**celery, carrot and onion**, finely diced
1	**bay leaf**
½	**clove garlic**
250 g	**cannellini beans**
	vegetable stock, as needed
5 g	**salt**
100 ml	**double (heavy) cream**
	freshly ground black pepper

Heat the olive oil in a large pan and sauté the diced vegetables with the bay leaf and garlic. Add the beans and cover with vegetable stock. Simmer until the beans are fully cooked. Purée about 60 g of the braised beans, then push through a fine-mesh sieve (strainer). Adjust the salt and cream, then season with pepper. Transfer the mixture to a 1-litre siphon and keep warm in a bain-marie.

FOR THE TARRAGON OIL
100 g **tarragon leaves**
40 g **extra-virgin olive oil**
60 g **sunflower oil**

Blend all the ingredients together for 2–3 minutes, then strain through a microfibre cloth into a bowl. Set aside in a cool place away from direct sources of light and heat. This will result in a clear, brightly coloured oil with an intense aroma.

ASSEMBLY
Spread a nut-sized portion of sea urchin emulsion in the middle of a serving dish. Add some braised beans and two fresh sea urchin tongues. Cover with warm foam, drizzle with tarragon oil and garnish with wood sorrel leaves. On the side, arrange the crispy potato wafers, some more fresh sea urchin tongues and the oyster leaf strips.

Lombardy-style frog soup and fried frogs

Makes 20–22 spheres

FOR THE CRUMB COATING
100 g **washed and boiled Carnaroli rice**, drained well
60 ml **water**
9 g **salt**
3 g **soy sauce**
3 ml **white wine**
1 **clove garlic**
cloves, cinnamon, black peppercorns
200 g **boiled pork rind**

Spread the rice out over a sheet of baking (parchment) paper and dry out in the oven at 55°C/131°F overnight. Make a marinade by combining the water, the salt, soy sauce, white wine, garlic and spices. Add the pork rind and allow to marinate in the fridge overnight. The next day, wipe off the marinade and dry out the rind in the oven at 55°C/131°F overnight until crispy and translucent. Crush the rind into crumbs and mix it with the dried rice.

FOR THE FROG CROQUETTE MIXTURE
12 g **unsalted butter**
1 **sage leaf**
175 g **frog meat**
1 **tablespoon Marsala wine**
30 ml **double (heavy) cream**
15 g **mascarpone cheese**
1 **teaspoon grated Parmigiano Reggiano cheese**
1 **teaspoon chopped parsley or chives**
salt

Melt the butter in a frying pan or skillet with the sage leaf. Add the frog meat and gently brown, then deglaze with the Marsala. Season with salt, then mix in the cream and mascarpone. Take off the heat, remove and discard the sage and allow to cool. Transfer to a mixer and combine well, incorporating the Parmesan and herbs. Use a spherical mould to shape 10–12-g portions of the mixture into balls.

FOR THE FROG STOCK
2 kg **frog trunks** (head and legs removed)
extra-virgin olive oil, for cooking
500 ml **red wine**
2 **bunches each rosemary, sage and parsley stalks**
125 g **dried porcini mushrooms**, rehydrated and sautéed with garlic, salt and black pepper
250 g **celery**, chopped
250 g **celeriac (celery root)**, peeled and chopped
250 g **fennel bulb**, chopped
5 litres **water**
1 **smoked herring**

In a large pan, gently brown the frog trunks in olive oil, then add the wine and herbs. Reduce the liquid by half, add the sautéed mushrooms and chopped vegetables and allow them to absorb the flavours. Add the water and smoked herring, then bring to the boil and cook for 20 minutes. Pass the contents of the pan through a food mill then a fine-mesh sieve (strainer) into a clean pan and reduce the resulting stock by half. Set aside.

FOR THE FROG AND RICOTTA SOUP
80 g **celery, carrot and onion**, finely diced
extra-virgin olive oil, for cooking
½ **clove garlic**
1 **bay leaf**
200 g **buffalo ricotta cheese**
400 g **frog stock** (see above)
salt and ground black pepper

In a pan, sauté the diced vegetables in olive oil with the garlic clove and bay leaf. Add the ricotta and allow it to absorb the flavours, then add the stock. Season with salt and pepper. Cook, stirring regularly, until the soup is medium-thick, glossy and fragrant.

FOR THE PINK PICKLING LIQUOR GEL
125 ml **white wine**
90 g **white onion**
75 ml **raspberry vinegar**
50 ml **white vinegar**
25 g **acacia honey**
10 ml **red shallot vinegar**
5 g **ground white pepper**
1 **bay leaf**
1 **sage leaf**
200 ml **water**
agar-agar, as needed

In a large pan, combine all the ingredients, except the agar-agar, with the water and bring to the boil. Cover, turn off the heat and allow to steep for 10 minutes. Strain and weigh the resulting liquid. Add 1 g agar-agar for every 100 g of pickling liquor. Allow to set in the fridge, then blend to a soft and smooth gel.

FOR THE WILD GARLIC OIL
300 g **wild garlic**, washed and dried
400 g **extra olive oil**
400 g **sunflower oil**

Combine the ingredients in a Thermomix and blend for 7 minutes on the highest speed setting. Strain through muslin (cheesecloth) without pressing. Set aside.

ASSEMBLY
In a large bowl, make a thick batter by mixing equal measures of water, rice flour and rice starch. Dip the frog croquette balls into the batter, draining the excess batter, then roll them in the crumb coating until coated all over. Heat enough oil for deep-frying in a large deep pan to 180°C/350°F, or until a cube of bread browns in 30 seconds. Deep-fry the croquettes in the oil, then drain on kitchen paper (paper towels) and keep warm. Add a generous tablespoon of frog and ricotta soup to the middle of a serving plate. Arrange a croquette in the centre and finish with a few drops of the pickling liquor gel and the wild garlic oil.

Oysters and lardo

Serves 10

2	**fresh persimmons**
10	**walnut-glazed lardo oysters** (see below)
	extra-virgin olive oil, for brushing after oysters
	Maldon sea salt
10	**roasted walnuts** (see below)
18 g	**dill oil** (see below)

FOR THE LARDO OYSTERS

70 g	**Fine de Claire oysters**
5 g	**parsley stalk**
10 g	**shallot**
10 g	**extra-virgin olive oil**, plus extra to cover oysters
30 g	**cooked pork meat and back fat**
2 g	**chopped garlic**
5 g	**chopped chervil and chives**
	Maldon sea salt

Open the oysters and collect the liquor (set aside for the following step). Vacuum-seal the oysters in a bag with a parsley stalk, a small piece of shallot and enough olive oil to cover. Cook sous-vide in a steam oven at 58°C/136°F for 30 minutes, then cool the bag in iced water. Using a sharp knife, finely chop the pork meat and fat, and the cooked oysters. Season the mixture with the garlic, chopped herbs and extra-virgin olive oil. Fill specific oyster-shaped moulds and freeze.

FOR THE WALNUT-GLAZED LARDO OYSTER

20 ml	**milk**
10 g	**nocino (green walnut) liqueur reduction**
20 ml	**oyster liquor**
20 ml	**double (heavy) cream**
3.2 g	**kappa carrageenan per 100 g glaze mixture**

In a pan, combine the milk, liqueur, oyster liquor and cream, bring to the boil, then add the kappa carrageenan and stir until it has dissolved. Dip the frozen oysters into the kappa solution so they are lightly glazed all over, then set aside in the fridge until completely thawed.

FOR THE ROASTED WALNUTS

150 ml	**milk**
50 ml	**water**
10	**shelled walnut kernels**
	extra-virgin olive oil, for seasoning
0.3 g	**salt**

In a medium pan, bring the milk and water to the boil. Add the walnuts and simmer for 30 minutes. Drain the walnuts, quickly rinse and season with olive oil and the salt. Roast the walnuts in a convection oven at 160°C/325°F for 20 minutes, turning them halfway through cooking. This will give the walnuts a much more crumbly and fragrant texture when chewed, as most of their oil will have been lost when cooked in the liquid.

FOR THE DILL OIL

150 g	**dill leaves**
200 ml	**sunflower oil**
200 ml	**extra-virgin olive oil**

Combine all the ingredients in a Thermomix and heat to 70°C/158°F. Once the temperature has been reached, blend on the highest speed setting for a few minutes. Strain the oil through muslin (cheesecloth) and allow to cool as quickly as possible to preserve its bright colour and fresh aroma.

ASSEMBLY

Cut the persimmons open and remove the segments of firm pulp. Press the remainder of the fruit through a fine-mesh sieve (strainer) to remove the skin, stalk and the white core, which is the most astringent part. Add a scant tablespoon of persimmon purée to the middle of a serving dish and place a persimmon segment in the centre. Arrange a glazed lardo oyster on the persimmon segment, brush with olive oil for added gloss and season with salt flakes. Arrange 4 roasted walnut kernels on the dish and finish with a drizzle of dill oil.

Surf and turf: crayfish, mushrooms and catmint oil

Serves 4

FOR THE CRAYFISH AND MUSHROOM SAUCE

Part 1: Crayfish stock

250 g	**unsalted butter**
150 g	**celeriac (celery root)**, chopped
150 g	**celery**, chopped
150 g	**leek**, trimmed and chopped
150 g	**white mushrooms**, chopped
1,5 kg	**crayfish heads**
150 ml	**Cognac**
50 g	**tomato purée (paste)**
25 g	**dried porcini mushrooms**
1	**bulb garlic**
2	**whole cloves**
1	**star anise**
20 g	**parsley stalks**
150 g	**San Marzano tomatoes**
5 litres	**water**

Heat the butter in a large pan and sauté the vegetables, then remove and set aside. Add the crayfish heads to the pan and sauté until brown, then deglaze with the Cognac and add the previously sautéed vegetables. Add the tomato purée (paste), mushrooms, garlic, cloves, star anise, parsley and tomatoes. Cover with the water and cook for 40 minutes. Turn off the heat and allow the stock to settle for 1 hour. Strain the stock through a fine-mesh sieve (strainer), pressing the crayfish heads to extract all the juices.

part 2: Crayfish and mushroom sauce

1	**knob of butter**
100 g	**celery**, chopped
100 g	**leek**, trimmed and chopped
100 g	**white mushrooms**, chopped
100 g	**celeriac (celery root)**, chopped
1	**clove garlic**
	crayfish stock (see above)

Heat the butter in a large pan over a high heat and sauté the chopped vegetables and garlic. Add the stock and cook for a further 30 minutes. Blend everything together, then strain through a fine-mesh sieve (strainer) into a clean pan and heat until the sauce is reduced to the desired consistency.

ASSEMBLY

2	**fresh porcini mushrooms**
	zest and juice of 1 lemon
	extra-virgin olive oil, for seasoning
12	**mint leaves**, plus extra to serve
12	**catmint leaves**, plus extra to serve
12	**boiled crayfish tails**
10 g	**parsley oil**
	Maldon sea salt and ground white pepper

Cut the porcini mushrooms into 5-mm-/¼-inch-thick slices and blanch in a small pan of water with a little lemon juice for 15–20 seconds. Drain and season the mushroom slices with olive oil, sea salt and white pepper. Tear a mint leaf and a catmint leaf into small pieces and mix in well. Put 3 tablespoons of the crayfish and mushroom sauce on a serving plate and arrange the crayfish tails on top. Season with parsley oil, lemon zest, torn mint and catmint leaves and a few seasoned porcini mushroom slices.

Soft plankton buns and mustard caviar

Serves 10

10	**soft plankton buns** (see below)
30 g	**green tomato butter**
50 g	**mustard caviar** (see below)
20 g	**pink pickling liquor gel** (see page 199)
	chives and chervil leaves, to garnish

FOR THE SOFT PLANKTON BUNS

9 g	**fresh yeast**
12 ml	**water**
175 g	**soft wheat flour** (W index 180–230)
4 g	**malt flour**
5 g	**freeze-dried plankton**
18 g	**extra-virgin olive oil**, plus extra for brushing
180 ml	**milk**

In a small bowl, dissolve the yeast in the water. In a mixer, combine the flours and plankton, turn it on, then add the olive oil, milk and yeast mixture and mix for 5–7 minutes to form a dough with good structure and a smooth texture. Leave the dough to rest at room temperature for 15 minutes, then divide it into 22-g portions. Gather each portion into a ball by rotating and compacting it with your hands, then place it on perforated baking trays. Leave the buns to prove at room temperature until they have doubled in size, then brush the tops with oil and bake in a steam oven at 110°C/230°F for 18 minutes. Allow to cool with baking trays placed on top of the buns to keep the tops flat, then set aside in the fridge.

FOR THE MUSTARD CAVIAR

250 g	**white mustard seeds**
1.5 litres	**Barbecued white fish stock** (see page 205)
5 g	**fresh squid ink**
15 g	**katsuobushi (bonito flakes)**
1 g	**cornflour (cornstarch)**
1	**teaspoon water**
5 ml	**extra-virgin olive oil**

In a pan, boil the mustard seeds four times, starting with cold water and changing the water each time, skimming the cooking water and allowing the seeds to simmer for 25 minutes each time. In another pan, heat the fish stock to 80–90°C/176–194°F, then add the squid ink and katsuobushi. Allow to steep for 5 minutes, then strain into a clean pan. Add the mustard seeds to the stock and cook gently until the stock has been completely absorbed by the seeds. In a small bowl, dissolve the cornflour (cornstarch) in the water, then stir in the slurry. Drizzle with the olive oil for a gloss, allow to cool, then set aside in the fridge.

ASSEMBLY

Cut off the top of each bun transversely and toast the cut surface in a frying pan or skillet with a knob of butter. Allow to cool, then spread with green tomato butter. Sprinkle with the mustard caviar and finish with two or three drops of shallot gel, two chives and a chervil leaf.

Soft squash buns and trout

Serves 10

10	**soft squash buns** (see below)
120 g	**sweet-and-sour squash cream** (see below)
40 g	**mustard seeds with squash and turmeric** (see below)
25 g	**soy sauce and lime-marinated squash**
150 g	**marinated trout**
20 g	**pumpkin seed crumble** (see below)

FOR THE SOFT SQUASH BUNS

5 g	**fresh yeast**
70 ml	**fresh squash juice**
40 g	**egg** (for the dough)
100 g	**squash, cooked en papillote and mashed**
250 g	**soft wheat flour** (W index 180–230)
25 g	**caster (superfine) sugar**
5 g	**salt**
50 g	**unsalted butter**, cut into small pieces and slightly softened
40 g	**egg** (for brushing)
10 ml	**double (heavy) cream**

In a bowl, dissolve the yeast in the squash juice at room temperature. In another bowl, mix the 40 g egg and mashed squash together. Put the flour into a mixer, turn it on and add the squash juice and yeast mixture. Mix until a dough forms, then incorporate the egg and squash mixture, a third at a time. Add the sugar and salt. When the dough is smooth, incorporate the butter a little at a time. Cover the dough and allow it to rest in the fridge overnight. The next day, gently knead the dough on a work surface by stretching and folding it, taking care not to overwork it and allow it to develop structure. Divide the dough into 25-g portions and gather each portion into a ball by rotating and compacting it with your hands. Place the dough balls on perforated baking trays. Beat the remaining egg and cream together in a small bowl, then brush this egg wash over the buns. Allow to rise at room temperature until doubled in size, then brush with more egg wash and bake in a steam oven at 110°C/230°F for 14 minutes. Allow to cool with baking trays placed on top of the buns to keep the tops flat.

FOR THE MUSTARD SEEDS WITH SQUASH AND TURMERIC

30 g	**cooked mustard seeds**
20 ml	**fresh squash juice**
1 g	**fresh turmeric juice**
0.5 g	**salt**
0.5 g	**acacia honey**
0.5 ml	**apple cider vinegar**
30 ml	**water**

In a large pan, bring all the ingredients and the water to a gentle boil and reduce to the desired density. Allow to cool.

FOR THE SWEET-AND-SOUR SQUASH CREAM

225 g	**red kuri squash**
12 ml	**white wine vinegar**
12 g	**caster (superfine) sugar**
30 g	**white miso paste**
1,5 g	**salt**
2 ml	**soy sauce**
2	**whole cloves**
2	**juniper berries**
½	**bay leaf**
½	**clove garlic**

Cook the squash in a large pan with the remaining ingredients (put the aromatics into a bouquet garni bag) until tender. Remove and discard the bouquet garni and purée in a blender to a smooth and consistent cream.

FOR THE PUMPKIN SEED CRUMBLE

50 g	**pumpkin seeds**
10 g	**unsalted butter**
50 g	**crushed amaretti biscuits (cookies)**
	salt

In a frying pan or skillet, toast the pumpkin seeds in the butter, then season with salt. Drain on kitchen paper (paper towels) and allow to cool. Mix the toasted seeds with the crushed amaretti in a small bowl. We also like to dry the pulp from the squash that we juice for other dishes and add it powdered to the crumble for even more flavour. Depending on the strength of the squash powder in this case, adjust the flavour of the crumble to taste without the need for measuring it on scales.

ASSEMBLY
Thinly slice the red kuri squash and marinate them in enough olive oil, lime juice and soy sauce to cover. Cut the trout into 5-mm-/¼-inch-thick slices and brush with olive oil for gloss. Heat the squash buns by steaming. Using a small serrated knife, make a V-shaped cut in the middle of the top of the buns, remove the bread and fill the cavity with the sweet-and-sour squash cream and mustard seeds. Finish by alternating three slices of trout with three slices of marinated squash. Sprinkle with pumpkin seed crumble and serve lukewarm.

Bread, polenta and bruscitt'

Serves 10

FOR THE BRUSCITT' (STEWED BEEF FOR STUFFING)

250 g	**stewing steak**
25 g	**aged lardo (cured pork back fat)**
25 g	**unsalted butter**
1½	**teaspoons finely chopped white onion**
½	**clove garlic**, halved
1	**teaspoon fennel seeds**
1	**bay leaf**
250 ml	**red wine**
100 ml	**beef stock**
1	**star anise**
1	**tablespoon chopped dill**
	salt and ground black pepper

Mince (grind) the beef using a coarse plate on a mincer (grinder). Cook the meat, in batches, in a large pan until browned all over, then remove from the heat and set aside. Chop the lardo and melt in another large pan with half of the butter. In another pan, melt the remaining butter. Add the finely chopped onion and the melted butter to the lardo and sauté until the onion is coloured. Add the meat (browned separately), garlic, fennel seeds and bay leaf with salt and pepper. Deglaze with the red wine. When the caramelized juices have been dissolved, add the stock, star anise and dill and simmer for at least 2 hours. Cook until the liquid has reduced and the meat is glazed, then add the chopped fennel and turn off the heat. Allow to cool, then set aside in the fridge.

FOR THE POLENTA BREAD (makes 1 loaf)

18 g	**fresh yeast**
125 ml	**water**
35 g	**extra-virgin olive oil**
320 g	**soft wheat flour** (W index 180–230)
50 g	**buckwheat flour**
32 g	**caster (superfine) sugar**
6 g	**salt**
6 g	**powdered milk**
30 g	**whole egg**
35 g	**unsalted butter**, diced and chilled
100 g	**cooked firm yellow polenta**
1	**egg yolk**
	a little double (heavy) cream
	Maldon sea salt

In a medium bowl, dissolve the yeast in the water and the olive oil. Combine the flours, sugar, salt and powdered milk in a mixer and mix on low speed, adding the whole egg, then add the yeast mixture. Once a dough is formed that shows good structure, add the cold butter in small pieces. Using your hands, break up the polenta and incorporate it into the dough. Allow the dough to rest at room temperature for 30 minutes, then divide it into 20-g balls. Stuff each ball with 12–15 g of bruscitt' (stewed beef), taking care to seal the filling well inside the dough. Position the stuffed dough balls in a 22-cm/8½-inch cake tin (pan) with the sides touching and prove for 1 hour at 27°C/81°F. Mix the egg yolk and cream together, then brush the loaf with the egg wash. Bake in a steam oven at 100°C/212°F for 18 minutes. Allow to cool, then brush the top again with more egg wash, sprinkle with sea salt flakes and bake in a steam oven at 200°C/392°F for 9 minutes. Remove from the oven and allow to rest for a few minutes before serving.

FOR THE RED WINE REDUCTION

2 litres	**red wine**
100 g	**shallots**, chopped
100 g	**carrot**, chopped
100 g	**celery**, chopped
1	**bay leaf**
25 g	**honey** (optional)

Bring the wine to the boil in a large pan, then set alight to it and flambé until all the alcohol evaporates. Add the chopped vegetables and bay leaf and allow to reduce. You can also add the honey halfway through, if you like. Once the reduction is smooth, glossy and thick, turn off the heat and set aside.

FOR THE VEGETABLE SAUCE WITH RED WINE AND FENNEL

30 g	**red wine reduction** (see above)
250 g	**Vegetable sauce** (see page 203)
1	**knob of cold butter**
1	**tablespoon finely chopped fresh dill**

Add the red wine reduction to the vegetable sauce in a large pan, reduce a little if necessary, then whisk in the cold butter for gloss. Add the chopped dill to the sauce immediately before serving.

TO SERVE
After baking and resting for a few minutes, serve the whole loaf. At the table, divide it into individual portions and serve one to each diner on a small bread plate. Accompany with 2–3 heaped tablespoons of the well-heated sauce, leaving it up to the diner's personal preference to dip the stuffed bread into the sauce before eating.

Love in Portofino: Basil pesto, green beans and griddled potatoes

Serves 10

10	**crisp potato wafers**
350 g	**vegetable filling** (see below)
3 g	**miso powder**
150 g	**basil pesto** (see below)
25 g	**toasted pine nuts**

BASIL PESTO

100 g	**fresh basil leaves**
35 g	**extra-virgin olive oil**
20 g	**pine nuts**
2 g	**salt**
1	**small clove garlic**

For blending

10 g	**Parmigiano Reggiano cheese**, grated
10 g	**pecorino cheese**, grated
10 g	**extra-virgin olive oil**

Make a traditional pesto with the first five ingredients and blend in the cheese and additional olive oil just before mixing with the vegetables.

FOR THE VEGETABLE FILLING

70 g	**mangetout (snow peas)**, cut into 1-cm/½-inch dice
70 g	**flat beans**, cut into 1-cm/½-inch dice
70 g	**French (green) beans**, cut into 1-cm/½-inch dice
70 g	**tromboncino squash**, cut into 1-cm/½-inch dice
20 g	**extra-virgin olive oil**
70 g	**potatoes**, cut into 5-mm/¼-inch dice
	reserved basil pesto (see above)

Sauté the mangetout (snow peas), beans and squash separately in a frying pan or skillet in a teaspoon of extra-virgin olive oil until tender. Parboil the diced potatoes in a small pan and finish cooking them on a griddle (grill pan) until golden on all sides. Mix the vegetables together in a bowl, then add the pesto and mix until everything is combined.

ASSEMBLY
Immediately before serving, dip a potato wafer into some boiling water for a few seconds then place it on a work surface. Place some of the vegetable and pesto mixture on the top of the wafer and carefully roll it up, folding in the ends to keep in the filling. Toast the surface with a blowtorch and sprinkle with miso powder. Finish with a dab of pesto and three toasted pine nuts.

Vegetable sauce for dipping

Serves 8

500 g	**white mushrooms**, trimmed and cut into uniform dice
500 g	**San Marzano tomatoes**, cut into uniform dice
2 kg	**Jerusalem artichokes**, cleaned and cut into uniform dice
1 kg	**celeriac (celery root)**, peeled and cut into uniform dice
500 g	**celery**, cut into uniform dice
250 g	**shallots**, cut into uniform dice
2	**cloves garlic**
1	**bay leaf**
5 g	**thyme**
10 g	**tomato purée (paste)**
5 kg	**ice cubes**
100 ml	**Marsala wine**
100 g	**black truffle water**
100 g	**smoked butter**
30 g	**Red wine reduction** (see page 202)
	salt and ground black pepper
	herb oil
	bread, to serve
	extra-virgin olive oil, for drizzling

Roast the mushrooms, tomatoes, Jerusalem artichokes, celeriac (celery root), celery and shallots in the oven at 185°C/365°F for 1 hour. Transfer the vegetables to a large pan and add the garlic, bay leaf and thyme. Add the tomato purée and cover everything with the ice and bring to the boil, then reduce the heat and simmer for 45 minutes. Strain into a clean pan and cook until it is reduced by two-thirds. Add the Marsala and truffle water and adjust the seasoning with salt and pepper. Stir in the smoked butter for a glossy, thick and smooth sauce.
Serve the vegetable sauce with a few drops of herb oil, accompanied by a piece of irregularly shaped bread, which is drizzled with oil and lightly toasted on a griddle (grill pan).

Aubergine carpaccio alla Norma

Serves 4

360 g	**aubergine carpaccio** (see below)
30 g	**smoked scamorza gel**
60 g	**Norma sauce** (see below)
15 g	**pecorino cheese**, grated
	oregano shoots, as needed
	basil shoots, as needed
	marjoram shoots, as needed
35 g	**toasted breadcrumbs**
	extra-virgin olive oil
	Maldon sea salt and ground black pepper

FOR THE AUBERGINE CARPACCIO

2	**seedless aubergines (eggplants)**
280 ml	**mozzarella whey**

Peel the aubergines (eggplants) and cut off the stalks. Vacuum-seal in a bag with the mozzarella whey and cook sous-vide in a steam oven at 120°C/248°F for 35 minutes. Allow to cool, then thinly slice using a mandoline. Set aside in the fridge.

SMOKED SCAMORZA GEL

200 ml	**water**
125 ml	**milk**
175 g	**smoked scamorza cheese**, cut into pieces
	agar-agar, as needed
	salt and ground black pepper

In a large pan, heat the water and the milk together to 60°C/140°F. Transfer to a Thermomix and add the cheese. Run the Thermomix on medium speed and set the temperature to 55°C/131°F, then blend on the highest speed setting. Once the temperature has been reached, strain the liquid through a sieve (strainer) and season with salt and pepper. Add 0.8 g of agar-agar for every 100 g of liquid and dissolve. Allow to cool and set in the fridge. Cut the jelly into pieces and blend to a smooth gel.

FOR THE NORMA SAUCE

	oil, for deep-frying
200 g	**Viola aubergine (eggplant)**, diced
300 g	**cooked datterini tomato sauce**
10 g	**assorted basil, marjoram and oregano leaves**
30 g	**Parmigiano Reggiano cheese**, grated
50 ml	**extra-virgin olive oil**
	salt and ground black pepper

Heat enough oil for deep-frying in a large, deep pan to 180°C/350°F, or until a cube of bread browns in 30 seconds. Carefully add the aubergine (eggplant) to the hot oil and deep-fry until golden. Remove with a slotted spoon and drain on kitchen paper (paper towels). Bring the datterini tomato sauce to a simmer in a pan, then add the aubergine and continue to simmer for 40 minutes. To finish, add the herbs and allow their aromas to infuse. Using an immersion blender, whisk the sauce, gradually adding the grated cheese and olive oil until the sauce is thick and emulsified. Season with salt and pepper.

ASSEMBLY
Arrange the aubergine carpaccio overlapped in the middle of a serving plate and season with scamorza gel and Norma sauce. Place a heaped teaspoon of grated pecorino cheese to one side, as well as fragrant herb shoots and crispy toasted breadcrumbs. Finish by drizzling with olive oil and seasoning with sea salt.

Avocado, kiwi and coriander

Serves 6

2	**avocados**
50 ml	**extra-virgin olive oil**, plus extra for drizzling
10 ml	**lime juice**
6	**drops Tabasco sauce**
2	**fresh kiwis** (not too ripe)
500 g	**fresh coriander (cilantro)**
1 g	**agar-agar**, as needed
20 g	**tuna bottarga**, thinly sliced
6	**nasturtium leaves**
8	**wild rocket (arugula) leaves**
	salt

Cut open the avocados, remove the stone (pit) and scoop out the flesh. Cut the flesh into chunks and combine in a blender with the olive oil, salt, lime juice and Tabasco sauce. Blend to a smooth, creamy purée. Peel and cut the kiwis into 1–2-cm/½–¾-inch dice. Pick the coriander (cilantro), setting aside 10 g of the fleshiest stalks and about 10 of the tenderest leaves. Blanch the remaining coriander leaves in a small pan of lightly salted water, then blend to a smooth purée. Measure out 1 g of agar-agar for every 100 g of coriander purée and dissolve. Spread a thin layer of purée over a small tray to make a sheet of coriander jelly.

ASSEMBLY
Mix the kiwi and avocado purée together in a bowl. Add the finely chopped coriander stalks and three or four coriander leaves, torn into small pieces. Place a portion of this mixture in the middle of a serving plate and garnish the top with two thin slices of bottarga, some coriander, nasturtium and wild rocket (arugula) leaves lightly drizzled with olive oil for gloss. Finish by placing a thin disc of coriander jelly on top.

Sole alla cacciatora

Serves 4

FOR THE SOLE BALLOTINES

125 g	**sole fillet**, minced
10 g	**egg white**
75 ml	**cold double (heavy) cream**
135 g	**red (bell) peppers**, finely diced
135 g	**white mushrooms**, finely diced
	extra-virgin olive oil, for cooking
100 g	**pork caul fat**
20 g	**assorted seaweed**, rehydrated
2	**sole fillets**, cleaned and cut in half
	fish stock, to cover
5 g	**mustard**
	salt and ground white pepper

Make a basic forcemeat by blending the sole flesh with the egg white and pressing it through a sieve (strainer). Season with salt and pepper. Incorporate the cold cream and set aside in the fridge. Sauté the peppers and mushrooms separately in a frying pan or skillet in a little oil. Allow to cool, then mix the vegetables with the forcemeat until combined. Adjust the seasoning with salt. Spread the caul fat inside 6–7-cm-/2½–2¾-inch-diameter hemisphere moulds. Fill each mould with 5 g of rehydrated seaweed and cover with a teaspoon of the forcemeat. Roll up a half fillet of sole and press it into the centre of the forcemeat. Cover with a little more of the forcemeat and wrap everything tightly in the overhanging caul fat to make compact and well-rounded ballotines. Cook the ballotines in fish stock at 70°C/158°F for 15 minutes.

FOR THE FISH CACCIATORE SAUCE
Step 1 (Sauce base)

200 g	**chicken wings**
	extra-virgin olive oil, for cooking and roasting
3	**celery sticks (stalks)**, chopped
2	**red (bell) peppers**, chopped
100 g	**white mushrooms**, chopped
⅓	**leek**, trimmed and chopped
2	**red onions**, chopped
3	**spring onions (scallions)**, chopped
2	**cloves garlic**, chopped
100 g	**datterini tomatoes**, chopped
30 g	**parsley stalks**
10 g	**dried porcini mushrooms**, rehydrated in a little water
200 l	**red wine**
100 g	**langoustine heads**, eyes and brains removed
1 kg	**soup fish (rockfish, cod, red mullet)**, cleaned and gills and eyes removed
80 g	**tomato purée (paste)**
100 g	**clam liquor**
5 kg	**ice cubes**
1	**bunch basil**
1 litre	**water**

Roast the chicken wings in the oven at 200°C/400°F, drizzling just a little oil to remove the fat and brown them well. In a large pot, sauté the celery, peppers, mushrooms, leeks, onions and spring onions with the garlic and tomatoes over medium heat. Add the roast chicken wings, parsley stalks and dried mushrooms. Deglaze with red wine. Add the cleaned langoustine heads, the fish, the tomato paste and the clam liquor. Pour in the water and cover with ice. Cook over a low heat for 1½ hours, and at the end of the cooking time, infuse with basil. Strain the mixture through a coarse-mesh sieve and set aside.

Step 2

1	**red (bell) pepper**, chopped
1	**white onion**, chopped
100 g	**datterini tomatoes**, halved
	extra-virgin olive oil, for cooking
100 ml	**dry white wine**
4 litres	**sauce base** (see above)
	pinch of cornflour (cornstarch), optional

Sauté the pepper, onion and tomatoes with olive oil in a large pan until coloured. Deglaze with the wine and allow the wine to reduce completely, then add the sauce base and cook for 45 minutes, or until it is reduced to the desired consistency. Whisk the finished sauce and thicken slightly with the cornflour (cornstarch), if necessary.
Sear the sole ballotines, browning the surface well and cooking the caul fat at the same time. Pat dry with kitchen paper (paper towels).

ASSEMBLY
Place a heaped tablespoon of the cacciatore sauce in the middle of a serving plate and arrange a ballotine in the centre. Serve piping hot.

Vicenza-style trout and bitter cocoa

Serves 6

18 g	**cacao buttons (100% cacao)** (25 mm/1 inch in diameter, 3 mm/⅛ inch thick)
6	**trout ballotines** (see below)
300 g	**vicentina sauce** (see below)

FOR THE TROUT BALLOTINES

125 g **white trout flesh and trimmings**
15 g **egg white**
50 ml **cold double (heavy) cream**
40 g **onion**, stewed and finely chopped
30 g **sweetcorn kernels**, steamed
30 g **salmon trout**, cut into small cubes
3 g **parsley**, chopped
100 g **pork caul fat**
90 g **white trout flesh**, cut into about 1-cm/½-inch cubes
salt and ground white pepper

Make a forcemeat by blending the 125 g trout flesh and trimmings with the egg white in a large bowl. Season with salt and pepper, then incorporate the cold cream and set aside in the fridge. Mix the remaining ingredients, except the caul fat and trout cubes, into the forcemeat until combined. If necessary, adjust the seasoning with salt and pepper. Spread the caul fat inside 6–7-cm-/2½–2¾-inch-diameter hemisphere moulds. Add a teaspoon of forcemeat to the middle of each mould, press a cube of white trout flesh into it and cover with another teaspoon of forcemeat. Wrap everything tightly in the overhanging caul fat to make compact and well-rounded ballotines. Cook in a large pan of water at 60°C/140°F for about 15 minutes.

FOR THE VICENTINA SAUCE

2 **white onions**, julienned
1 **clove garlic**, peeled and left whole
1 **bay leaf**
1 **parsley stalk**
225 g **extra-virgin olive oil**, plus extra for cooking
40 g **salted anchovies**
400 g **dried stockfish** (about 750 g final weight), sliced
625 ml **milk**
500 ml **double (heavy) cream**
8 **black peppercorns**
50 g **Parmigiano Reggiano cheese**, grated
10 g **sorrel leaves**, julienned

Preheat the oven to 180°C/350°F. In a large ovenproof pan with a lid, sauté the onions, garlic, bay leaf and parsley stalk in a little olive oil until lightly coloured. Add the anchovies and cook until dissolved, then add the sliced stockfish. Add the milk, 225 g olive oil and cream and gently bring to the boil. Add the peppercorns, cover the pan and cook for about 3 hours. Pour the contents of the pan into a colander set over a large bowl and collect the liquid. Whisk the sauce, incorporating the Parmesan, until thick, creamy and smooth. Before serving, add the sorrel to the sauce.

To serve, pan-fry the ballotines until they are golden. Pour the warmed sauce in the centre of each serving plate, place three cacao buttons on the sauce and a ballotine on top. Serve immediately.

Vignarola of home-grown vegetables with capers and bruscandoli

Serves 4

40 g **aged guanciale**, cut into small chunks
100 g **French beans**
100 g **asparagus spears**
100 g **flat beans**
80 g **podded broad (fava) beans**
80 g **freshly shelled peas**
100 g **baby artichokes**
extra-virgin olive oil, for cooking
2 **tablespoons water**
150 g **capers and wild hop shoot butter** (see below)
12 **pickled jasmine flowers**
12 **pea shoots**
salt and ground black pepper

FOR THE CAPER AND WILD HOP SHOOT BUTTER

20 g **shallot**, julienned
1 **tablespoon extra-virgin olive oil**
225 g **unsalted butter**, plus 2 knobs for cooking
1 **clove garlic**, peeled and left whole
150 g **wild hop shoots**, cleaned and finely diced
50 ml **stout beer**
25 g **capers**, desalted and puréed
salt and ground white pepper

Sauté the shallot in a pan with the oil, then add a knob of butter and the garlic and hop shoots and stir. Deglaze with the beer and continue to cook, spooning the liquid over from time to time. When the shoots are tender, add another knob of butter and season with salt and pepper. Remove and discard the garlic clove. Combine the braised shoots with the softened butter and puréed capers in a blender and blend until smooth, creamy and infused with the herbal, bitter and savoury notes of the other ingredients. Set aside. In a pan, gently brown the guanciale in its own fat until golden. Set aside. Gently sauté each vegetable separately in a frying pan or skillet with olive oil until coloured, then mix them together in another pan. Add the water and stir in the flavoured butter. Season with salt and pepper. The vegetables should be bright and glossy with a light coating of butter.

ASSEMBLY

Distribute the vegetables among serving plates and arrange 2 pieces of guanciale, 2 jasmine flowers and 3 fresh pea shoots on top.

Warm spaghetti with a barbecued fish, tomato and ginger sauce

Serves 4

FOR THE BARBECUED WHITE FISH STOCK

2,5 kg **white fish bones, flesh and trimmings**, roasted on a barbecue (grill)
1 **lemon**, charred on a barbecue (grill)
6-7 **sprigs rosemary**, charred on a barbecue (grill)
10 **spring onions (scallions)**, chopped
10 **celery sticks (stalks)**
500 g **fresh ginger**
1 **garlic bulb**
8 kg **ice cubes**
4 **smoked herring fillets**

Combine the roasted fish bones in a large saucepan. Add the vegetables and cover with the ice. Bring to the boil, then reduce the heat and simmer for 2 hours. Add the herring fillets and let infuse for 30 minutes. Strain into a clean pan, discarding solids, and reduce the resulting stock by two-thirds.

25 ml **fresh ginger juice**
120 g **Raw tomato sauce** (see page 216)
240 g **dried spaghetti**
200 ml **barbecued white fish stock** (see above)
extra-virgin olive oil
1 **celery stick (stalk)**, diced, plus torn celery leaves and extra leaves to garnish
5 g **colatura di alici (anchovy extract)**
10 g **dried caper seeds**, to garnish

Add the ginger juice to the tomato sauce, checking and adjusting the spiciness of the resulting sauce. Cook the spaghetti for 5 minutes less than the indicated cooking time. Drain and transfer to a large pan with the fish stock and finish cooking with the addition of olive oil, the celery stick (stalk), torn celery leaves and the anchovy extract.

ASSEMBLY
Twirl the spaghetti into nests and arrange in the middle of serving plates, then cover with the tomato and ginger sauce. Garnish with celery leaves and crunchy caper seeds.

Lumachine alla marinara with mussels and glasswort

Serves 6

1 **clove garlic**
20 g **parsley stalks and leaves**, torn
50 g **extra-virgin olive oil**
1 kg **ripe plums**, stoned (pitted) and cut into chunks
30 g **tomato purée (paste)**
15 g **light brown sugar**
40 ml **mussel liquor**
5 g **colatura di alici (anchovy extract)**
10 **basil leaves**
420 g **dried lumachine pasta**
180 g **mussels**, cleaned, steamed open and removed from shells
70 g **glasswort**
1 **tablespoon extra-virgin olive oil**
5 g **parsley powder**, for dusting
salt and ground white pepper

In a pan, sauté the garlic clove and parsley stalks in the 50 g olive oil until lightly coloured. Add the plums and allow them to heat through, then add the tomato purée (paste) and sugar. Season with salt, reduce the heat to low and simmer for about 40 minutes. Remove from the heat and pass the contents of the pan through a food mill. Return the purée to the pan and season with the mussel liquor, colatura di alici (anchovy extract), basil and pepper. Allow the flavours to infuse, then adjust the seasoning with salt, if necessary. Cook the pasta, then drain and stir it directly into the sauce. Add the mussels, glasswort, torn parsley leaves and the tablespoon of olive oil. As soon as the pasta is al dente and well coated in the sauce, serve it on plates, lightly dusted with parsley powder.

Mixed pasta in chestnut and mushroom soup with red wine, bay leaf and mascarpone

Serves 6

180 g **Gragnano mixed dried pasta**
250 g **chestnut and mushroom soup** (see below)
extra-virgin olive oil, for coating
15 g **coriander (cilantro)**, finely chopped
60 g **fresh mascarpone cheese**
40 g **bay leaf extract**
salt and ground black pepper

FOR THE CHESTNUT AND MUSHROOM SOUP
50 g **unsalted butter**
1 **clove garlic**, crushed
1 **bay leaf**
500 g **fresh porcini mushrooms**
150 g **cooked chestnuts**, chopped
50 ml **Marsala wine**
80 ml **red wine**
100 ml **mushroom stock**
salt and ground white pepper

In a pan, melt 25 g of the butter, add the crushed garlic, bay leaf, mushrooms and chopped chestnuts and sauté until coloured, then season with salt and pepper. Deglaze with the Marsala and reduce completely. Add the red wine and mushroom stock and cook for about 20 minutes without allowing the liquid to dry out. Finish by stirring in the knob of butter. Cook the pasta in a large pan of boiling salted water. Reheat the soup, then drain the pasta and add to the soup with olive oil and mix until well coated.

ASSEMBLY
Immediately before serving, add the chopped coriander (cilantro) to the pasta and season with plenty of pepper. Serve the pasta on plates, adding a teaspoon of fresh mascarpone and a tablespoon of bay leaf extract to the centre.

Buckwheat, apple and pork

Serves 4

80 g **buckwheat**
10 g **unsalted butter**, plus a knob for coating
25 g **dry white wine**
300 ml **hot pork stock** (see below)
40 g **pork rind**, boiled and cut into strips
30 g **cooked ham**, cut into small cubes
extra-virgin olive oil, for seasoning
20 g **pecorino cheese**, grated
2 g **finely chopped chives**
5 g **sage oil**
white wine vinegar, as needed

FOR THE PORK STOCK
750 g **ice cubes**
125 g **culatello trimmings**
70 g **toasted buckwheat**
60 g **smoked pancetta**
1 **white onion**
1 **celery stick (stalk)**
½ **carrot**
½ **celeriac (celery root)**
¼ **fresh chicken** (preferably thighs)
4 **black peppercorns**
1 **whole clove**
1 **juniper berry**
1 **bay leaf**
1 **blade mace**
3 **fennel seeds**
500 ml **water**

Put all the ingredients into a large pan with the water and bring to a simmer. Continue to simmer for 4 hours, then strain and set aside.

FOR THE BUCKWHEAT JELLY
800 ml **water**
300 g **toasted buckwheat**
50 g **spring onions (scallions)**, chopped
40 g **soy sauce**
10 ml **white wine vinegar**
4 g **agar-agar**

In a large pan, bring the water to the boil, add the toasted buckwheat and allow to steep for 10 minutes. Strain into a clean pan and reduce the liquid by half.

Spread the mixture over an acetate sheet to a thickness of 2–3 mm/1/16–1/8 inch. Once the jelly is set and cold, cut out a square sheet of the desired size.

FOR THE STUFFED SAGE LEAVES

100 g **rice flour**
100 g **soft wheat flour** (W index 180–230)
400 ml **sparkling water**
sunflower oil, for deep-frying
250 g **boiled pork snout trimmings**, finely chopped
25 g **veal jus**
2,5 g **salt**
zest of ½ lemon
8 **sage leaves**
ground white pepper

Make a thick and smooth tempura batter by mixing 1 part each of rice flour and soft wheat flour with 2 parts cold sparkling water. Heat enough sunflower oil for deep-frying in a large, deep pan to 180°C/350°F, or until a cube of bread browns in 30 seconds. Using a Japanese bamboo tea whisk, dip the whisk into the batter and allow droplets of the batter to fall directly into the hot oil. Make a good amount of fried batter bits and set aside on kitchen paper (paper towels). In a large bowl, mix the pork snout trimmings with the veal jus, add the salt and lemon zest and season with white pepper. Spread a teaspoon of the pork filling over a sage leaf, leaving a few millimetres free along the edges. Dab the edges with a layer of batter and place another sage leaf on top, then carefully press along the edges to seal the leaves together. Brush the stuffed leaves with more batter and coat them in the fried tempura bits. Reheat the oil for deep-frying, if necessary. Add the leaves to the hot oil and deep-fry for 2 minutes. Remove and drain on kitchen paper (paper towels) and set aside.

FOR THE APPLE SAUCE

1 **yellow apple**, peeled, cored and cut into pieces
1 **Fuji apple**, peeled, cored and cut into pieces
1 **Granny Smith apple**, peeled, cored and cut into pieces
1 **strip lemon zest**
1 **whole clove**
2 **black peppercorns**
salt

Combine all the ingredients in a vacuum bag and seal at 100% vacuum. Cook sous-vide by steaming at 85°C/185°F for 40 minutes. Remove and discard the aromatics and blend the apple sauce until smooth and thick. Toast the buckwheat in a frying pan or skillet with the 10 g butter. Deglaze with the white wine, then add half the hot pork stock and cook like a traditional risotto. After the first 5 minutes, add the pork rind strips and ham cubes. Continue cooking for a further 15 minutes, adding more stock from time to time. When finished, season with salt, pepper and olive oil. Add the chives and the knob of butter and stir until well coated, then fill cups for serving and add a few drops of sage oil. Cover the tops with a jelly sheet and garnish with a few drops of apple sauce. Accompany with the hot sage tempura.

La Milano che avanza: Marinated bread cutlet

Serves 6

3 **slices Black bread** (see page 272)
120 g **egg**, beaten
500 g **loaf sandwich bread**, crusts removed
400 g **clarified butter**
600 g **pickling liquor** (see below)
pickled red onion slices, as needed
Maldon sea salt

FOR THE PROTEIN SOAKING LIQUID

200 g **veal and pork trimmings**
5 g **soy sauce**
300 ml **reduced beef stock** (starting quantity: 600 ml)

The beef stock used as a base for the soaking liquid should be made using meat that is well seared to caramelize the outer surface, which provides a strong and distinct flavour once combined with the remaining ingredients. Sear the meat trimmings in a very hot frying pan or skillet while retaining all their juices. Press the browned meat with a potato masher to release the juices and add with the soy sauce to the reduced stock.

FOR THE PICKLING LIQUOR

250 ml **reduced beef stock** (starting quantity: 1 litre)
125 ml **dry white wine**
75 ml **white wine vinegar**
50 g **acacia honey**
10 **black peppercorns**
1 **bay leaf**
1 **sage leaf**
½ **white onion**
15 g **soy sauce**

In a pan, combine all the ingredients and heat to 90°C/194°F. Cover the pan with cling film (plastic wrap) and allow to steep for 15 minutes. Strain the liquid. Toast the black bread slices in the oven, then soak them in the protein soaking liquid, turning them from time to time. The bread should be soaked without becoming too soft, while absorbing all the meaty flavours in the liquid. Dip the soaked bread slices in beaten egg, then coat in the breadcrumbs made by pushing the sandwich bread through a medium-mesh sieve (strainer), like a classic Milanese veal cutlet. In a frying pan or skillet, fry the coated bread in the hot clarified butter, making sure to brown it evenly all over. Remove and pat dry with kitchen paper (paper towels), then allow to cool. When cold, soak the bread cutlets in the pickling liquor to infuse with the aromas until fully absorbed. Cut six 2-cm/¾-inch slices and position one in the middle of each serving plate. Cover with a layer of pickled onion slices and sprinkle with sea salt flakes.

Rabbit à la royale blanche

Serves 6

450 g **forcemeat** (see below)
1 **rabbit, boned**
6 litres **chicken stock**, to cover
300 g **white royale sauce** (see below)
6 g **mastic oil**

RABBIT À LA ROYALE BLANCHE

200 g **minced veal** (60%) **and rabbit meat** (40%)
90 g **fresh mascarpone cheese**
60 g **rabbit livers**
40 g **celeriac (celery root)**, boiled and finely diced
40 g **Renetta apple**, finely diced
20 g **pine nuts**
15 g **Parmigiano Reggiano cheese**
2 g **salt**
66 g **egg**
grated nutmeg, as needed
salt and ground black pepper

In a mixer, combine all the forcemeat ingredients, except the seasonings, and beat until smooth, without allowing the mixture to heat. Season with pepper and nutmeg. Vacuum-seal the mixture in a bag to compact. On a work surface, lay the rabbit out flat with the inner side facing upwards. Season with salt, then spread the forcemeat along the middle. Bring the edges over the filling and roll up into a smooth, even cylinder. Wrap the cylinder in damp baking (parchment) paper and tie with string. Place in a braising pan filled with the chicken stock to cover and cook in a dry oven for 5 hours at 85°C/185°F. After this time, remove from the oven and allow to cool in the cooking liquid.

FOR THE WHITE RABBIT STOCK

2.5 kg	**rabbit bones and trimmings**
175 g	**unsalted butter**
350 g	**white onion**, chopped
350 g	**white mushrooms**, cleaned
350 g	**celeriac (celery root)**, chopped
200 g	**leek**, cut into pieces
200 g	**celery sticks (stalks)**, chopped
½	**bulb garlic**
500 g	**chicken wings**
5	**bay leaves**
5	**sage leaves**
2 g	**ground white pepper**
4	**whole cloves**
0.5 g	**juniper berries**
375 ml	**white port**
2 litres	**almond milk**
1 litre	**chicken stock**
2,5 kg	**ice cubes**

Sear the rabbit bones and trimmings in a large frying pan or skillet with the butter until well coloured. Remove and set aside, then sauté the vegetables and garlic until slightly soft, then set aside. In a large pan, combine the vegetables and garlic, bones and trimmings, the chicken wings, herbs and spices. Place the pan over a high heat, then deglaze with half the port. Allow to reduce completely, then add the port. Reduce completely, then add the almond milk and chicken stock and cover with the ice. Bring to the boil and skim off the scum. Simmer for 7–8 hours, skimming regularly. Strain the stock through muslin (cheesecloth) and set aside.

FOR THE WHITE ROYALE SAUCE

50 g	**leek**, trimmed and chopped
50 g	**white mushrooms**, cleaned
50 g	**celeriac (celeriac)**, chopped
	oil, for cooking
100 ml	**white port**
2.5 litres	**white rabbit stock** (see above)

Sauté the vegetables in oil in a large pan until soft and coloured, then deglaze with the port and reduce completely. Add the rabbit stock and reduce by two-thirds. Blend the sauce until smooth and consistent.

ASSEMBLY

500 g	**white royale sauce** (see above)
100 g	**rabbit livers**
30 g	**white chocolate**
50 ml	**double (heavy) cream**
5 g	**apple cider vinegar**
	ground white pepper

Heat the sauce in a large pan, then remove from the heat and incorporate the livers using an immersion blender. Melt the chocolate in the sauce and whisk in the cream until smooth and glossy. Adjust the seasoning with vinegar and white pepper.
To serve, slice a medallion of stuffed rabbit, heat and place in the middle of a serving plate, then cover with plenty of the royale sauce. Finish by adding two drops of mastic oil.

Braised oxtail, cumin and cherries

Serves 10

500 g	**coda alla vaccinara (stewed oxtail)**, meat shredded
80 g	**pickled cherries**, cut into small pieces
20 g	**fresh cherries**
20 g	**coriander (cilantro) leaves**, torn
10	**soft chocolate biscuits** (see below)

FOR THE SOFT CHOCOLATE BISCUITS

50 ml	**fresh milk**
60 g	**unsalted butter**
10 g	**bitter cocoa powder**
50 g	**plain (all-purpose) flour**
20 g	**strong white bread flour**
120 g	**whole egg**
200 g	**egg yolk**
70 g	**dark chocolate** (at least 70% cocoa solids), melted at 42–43°C/108–109°F
200 g	**egg whites**
70 g	**caster (superfine) sugar**

In a large pan, cook a roux with the milk, butter, cocoa and flours. Transfer to a mixer and gradually incorporate the whole egg and yolk. Add the melted chocolate and mix until combined. Beat the egg whites with the sugar to stiff peaks, then fold them into the chocolate mixture until smooth. Using a rectangular stencil, spread the mixture over a silicone baking mat to a thickness of 4–5 mm (⅙–¼ inch). Bake in a steam oven for 10 minutes at 90°C/194°F. Store in the fridge.

FOR THE CODA ALLA VACCINARA (STEWED OXTAIL)

300 g	**celery**, finely diced
200 g	**white onions**, finely diced
50 g	**aged guanciale**, diced
2	**cloves garlic**, finely diced
	extra-virgin olive oil, for cooking
1 kg	**oxtail**, cut into sections
300 ml	**red wine**
30 g	**tomato purée (paste)**
300 g	**chopped tomatoes**
1l	**bouquet garni (rosemary, sage, laurel)**
500 ml	**beef stock**
50 g	**sultanas (golden raisins)**
50 g	**pine nuts**
15 g	**bitter cocoa powder**
15 g	**cocoa mass**
	salt and ground black pepper

In a large ovenproof pan with a lid, sauté 200 g of celery, the onions, guanciale and garlic in olive oil until the celery and onions are soft. In a large frying pan or skillet with a little oil, sear the meat until well browned. Add the browned meat to the vegetables, deglaze with the wine and add the tomato purée (paste), followed by the chopped tomatoes. Add the bouquet garni and enough stock to cover two-thirds of the contents of the pan. Cover with the lid and cook in the oven at 185°C/365°F for 1 hour. Turn the meat over, cover and continue to cook for 1 hour 30 minutes, removing the lid for the last 30 minutes to concentrate the aromas and juices. Check that the meat is cooked and falling off the bone. Remove from the oven and allow to rest with the lid on for 30 minutes. Take the meat out of the pan, remove the bones and shred the flesh. Remove and discard the bouquet garni and reduce the cooking liquid to a loose but consistent sauce. Add the remaining 100 g finely diced celery, the sultanas (golden raisins), pine nuts, cocoa powder and cocoa mass and adjust the seasoning with salt and pepper. Add the sauce to the shredded meat, then cool quickly in a blast chiller and set.

ASSEMBLY

Warm the oxtail and add the pickled cherries in small pieces, fresh cherries and some torn coriander (cilantro) leaves. Cover a soft biscuit with 50 g of oxtail and roll it up into a cylinder. Brush with the sauce for gloss and finish with more leaves. Serve.

Tender bone marrow and smoked almonds

Serves 6

90 g	**almond and smoked herring cream** (see below)
6	**lengths beef bone marrow**, thinly sliced
90 g	**blanched parsley**
	extra-virgin olive oil, for seasoning
18	**green almonds**
12 g	**smoked herring**
40 g	**parsley sauce** (see below)
10 g	**parsley oil** (see below)
	salt

FOR THE ALMONDS AND SMOKED HERRING CREAM

70 g	**blanched almonds**
150 ml	**unsweetened almond milk**
3 ml	**red shallot vinegar**
3 g	**salt**
15 ml	**herring oil** (see below)

Combine the almonds with the almond milk in a bag, vacuum-seal and refrigerate overnight. The next day, blend the contents of the bag with the vinegar, salt and herring oil to a thick and smooth sauce.

FOR THE HERRING OIL

250 g	**olive oil**
100 g	**smoked herring**

Combine the ingredients in a bag, vacuum-seal and steam at 70°C/158°F for 3 hours 30 minutes. Strain the oil. Set aside in the fridge.

FOR THE PARSLEY SAUCE

200 g	**parsley leaves**
300 ml	**sparkling water**

Blanch the parsley for 5 minutes in water and refresh in a bowl of iced water. Drain, then blend with the sparkling water until smooth and consistent. Strain through a fine-mesh sieve (strainer) and set aside.

ASSEMBLY
Place a tablespoon of almond and smoked herring cream in the middle of a serving plate and spread it out. On the cream, arrange 3 slices of bone marrow cooked under the salamander grill (broiler), 2 sprigs of blanched parsley seasoned with olive oil and salt, 3 almonds seasoned with olive oil, and 2 small pieces of smoked herring. Finish with 2–3 drops of parsley sauce and a drizzle of parsley oil before serving.

Pigeon and black pudding-stuffed cabbage

Serves 6

900 g	**black pudding forcemeat** (see below)
6	**skinless, boneless pigeon breasts**
6	**buckwheat crêpes** (see below)
20 g	**mustard**
12	**Savoy cabbage leaves**, blanched
40 g	**smoked pancetta**, cut into strips
100 g	**sweetcorn sauce** (see below)

FOR THE BLACK PUDDING FORCEMEAT

500 g	**minced (ground) meat** (45% veal, 45% pork, 10% pigeon livers)
200 g	**Milan-style black pudding (blood sausage)**
35 g	**sweet potato**, finely diced
35 g	**duck foie gras**
15 ml	**double (heavy) cream**
20 g	**soaked white bread**
10 g	**Parmigiano Reggiano cheese**, grated
3 g	**salt**
44 g	**egg yolk**
20 g	**mustard**
	ground cinnamon, as needed
	ground white pepper

Make a traditional forcemeat by blending the ingredients together, then set aside. Place a portion of forcemeat on a skinless pigeon breast. Brush both sides of the crêpes with mustard and wrap the forcemeat-covered breasts. Then wrap them in the cabbage leaves and vacuum-seal in bags.

FOR THE BUCKWHEAT CRÊPES

300 ml	**fresh milk**
100 ml	**water**
90 g	**buckwheat flour**
90 g	**soft wheat flour** (W index 180–230)
30 g	**unsalted butter**
1	**teaspoon chopped chervil and spring onion (scallion)**
1	**teaspoon salt**

Make a batter with the ingredients and cook traditional crêpes, making them a little thicker than usual.

SALSA DI MAIS

400 g	**cooked sweetcorn kernels**
150 ml	**water**
2 g	**parsley stalks**, chopped
1 g	**lemon zest**, finely diced
40 g	**chicken jus**
	salt

Blend the sweetcorn kernels with the water and salt. Press the mixture through a fine-mesh sieve (strainer), then cook to the consistency of a crème anglaise that is thick enough to coat a spoon. Immediately before serving, heat the sauce and add the parsley stalks, lemon zest and a few drops of chicken jus.

ASSEMBLY
When ready to serve, heat the wrapped pigeon breasts in the oven at 210°C/410°F for 9 minutes. Meanwhile, fry the pancetta in a frying pan or skillet and drain the excess oil on kitchen paper (paper towels). Serve the wrapped breast, to be sliced at the table with the pancetta and sweetcorn sauce.

Roasted bone marrow, saffron and gremolada

Serves 6

6	**veal femur marrow bones**, split lengthways
	extra-virgin olive oil, for drizzling
2	**sprigs rosemary**
1	**clove garlic**
120 g	**saffron gel** (see below)
60 g	**Milan-style gremolada** (see below)
	Maldon sea salt

FOR THE SAFFRON GEL

500 ml	**water**
30 g	**shallot**
½	**bay leaf**
2 g	**salt**
0.7 g	**saffron threads**
5 g	**agar-agar**

Combine all the ingredients, except the saffron and agar-agar, in a large pan. Bring to the boil and add the saffron. Turn off the heat, cover the pan with cling film (plastic wrap) and allow to steep for 20 minutes, then remove and discard the bay leaf and shallot. Add the agar-agar and bring to the boil. Transfer to a container and refrigerate until the jelly sets completely. Blend the now-stiff jelly to a smooth shiny and consistent gel. Set aside.

FOR THE MILAN-STYLE GREMOLADA

1	**orange**
1	**lemon**
100 g	**parsley leaves**
½	**clove garlic**

Peel the zest from the orange and lemon, removing all traces of pith, and finely dice. Using a knife, finely chop the parsley with the garlic and mix with the zest (although salted anchovy is sometimes added to the gremolada, we prefer not to use it). Set aside.

ASSEMBLY
In a baking dish, drizzle the marrow bones with olive oil and season with the rosemary. Roast at 200°C/400°F for 8 minutes. The marrow should be both firm and soft in the centre. Rest the marrow for 1 minute, rub the garlic clove on the hot bone in order to extract the aroma, then garnish with drops of saffron gel and a pinch of gremolada. Finish with sea salt and serve with a cappuccino spoon.

Pear, Gorgonzola dolce and mostarda

Serves 6

FOR THE PEAR SORBET

400 ml	**water**
325 g	**caster (superfine) sugar**
25 g	**muscovado sugar**
1	**bay leaf**
1	**whole clove**
5 g	**ground white pepper**
2 kg	**pear purée**
100 g	**dextrose**
50 g	**glucose syrup**
60 g	**glucose powder**

Make a syrup with the water, the sugars, bay leaf, clove and pepper. Strain and allow to cool, then mix with the pear purée until combined. Refrigerate the sorbet base overnight. The next day, churn the sorbet in a pacojet.

FOR THE GORGONZOLA FOAM

200 ml	**milk**
300 g	**Gorgonzola dolce cheese**

In a Thermomix, blend the milk with the cheese at 60°C/140°F for 5 minutes. Strain, transfer the mixture to a 500-g siphon and insert a nitrogen cartridge. Set aside.

50 g	**mostarda di Mantova (fruit and mustard condiment)**
1	**teaspoon finely chopped chives**
1	**teaspoon extra-virgin olive oil**
	ground white pepper

ASSEMBLY
Place 2–3 cubes of fruit from the mostarda in a glass, top with chives and drizzle with a little oil. Fill each glass to just over halfway with pear sorbet. Add more diced mostarda fruit and chives and fill to the top with the gorgonzola foam. Finish with 2 drops of olive oil and a sprinkling of pepper.

Strawberries and Fragolino

Serves 6

FOR THE STRAWBERRY SUGAR DISCS

300 g	**fondant brown sugar**
100 g	**glucose syrup**
100 g	**isomalt granules**
	oil, for greasing
20 g	**freeze-dried strawberries**

In a pan, combine the fondant sugar, glucose and isomalt. Boil to 160°C/320°F, then remove from the heat and pour the molten sugar over a lightly oiled Silpat. Wait for about 30 seconds, then sprinkle evenly with the freeze-dried strawberries. Using protective gloves, pull and stretch the sugar mass to incorporate the strawberries and give it a satin gloss. Once the sugar mass becomes mouldable, spread it out over the work surface and allow it to cool away from any sources of moisture and heat. Break up the cold caramel slab and grind to a powder in a blender. Using a sieve (strainer), spread the powder over a 6-cm-/2½-inch-diameter disc stencil laid on a Silpat. Lift off the stencil and melt the caramel powder with a kitchen blowtorch to make discs. Once cold, using a small palette knife, lift off the sugar discs and store in an airtight container with silica gel to keep them dry.

FOR THE STRAWBERRY JELLY

800 g	**fresh strawberries**, hulled
100 g	**wild strawberries**, hulled
100 g	**fresh raspberries**
50 g	**sugar**
	isinglass, as needed

Cut all strawberries and raspberries into chunks and blend with the sugar. Strain and weigh the juice obtained. Weigh out 4.5 g of isinglass for every 100 g of juice. Soak the isinglass in a bowl of cold water to rehydrate. In a pan, heat a tablespoon of juice to just over 40°C/104°F and dissolve the isinglass. Add the mixture to the remaining juice in a container, place over a bowl of ice water and allow to cool while stirring frequently, until completely set. Transfer to a piping (pastry) bag and store in the fridge.

FOR THE FRAGOLINO INFUSION

750 ml	**Fragolino wine**
100 g	**fresh raspberries**
20 g	**red shiso leaves**
50 g	**wild strawberries**, hulled
5 g	**raspberry vinegar**
2	**basil leaves**
2	**mint leaves**

Combine all the ingredients in a bag, vacuum-seal and allow to steep for 24 hours at 4°C/29°F. Strain the liquid and set aside in the fridge.

FOR THE STRAWBERRY AND ANGOSTURA BITTERS SORBET

500 g	**fresh strawberries**, hulled
90 g	**fructose**
50 g	**Angostura bitters**
4 g	**malic acid**

Blend all the ingredients until smooth and creamy. Pour into glasses and freeze. Pacotise immediately before serving.

ASSEMBLY

225 g	**wild strawberries**
18	**red shiso shoots**

Using a ring mould, pipe a ring of strawberry jelly on to a serving plate. Fill the centre with a portion of strawberry and Angostura bitters sorbet. Make a crown of wild strawberries around the sorbet. Decorate with 3 red shiso shoots and cover with a sugar disc.

At the table, complete the dish by pouring 2 heaped tablespoons of the Fragolino infusion over it.

Rice pudding arancini

Serves 6–8

80 g	**white chocolate**, chopped
15 g	**sunflower oil**, plus extra for deep-frying
300 g	**zabaglione inserts** (see below)
750 ml	**spice-infused milk** (see below)
140 g	**Carnaroli rice**
12 g	**caster (superfine) sugar**
80 g	**fresh mascarpone cheese**
100 g	**soft wheat flour** (W index 180–230)
4	**eggs**, beaten
400 g	**dried breadcrumbs**
	icing (confectioners') sugar, for dusting

FOR THE SPICE-INFUSED MILK

875 ml	**fresh milk**
½	**orange**
½	**lemon**
⅓	**cinnamon stick**
¼	**vanilla pod**
2	**cardamom pods**
2	**juniper berries**
1	**star anise**

In a large pan, combine all the ingredients and slowly bring to the boil. Remove from the heat, cover the pan with cling film (plastic wrap) and allow to steep for 10 minutes. Strain and set aside.

FOR THE ZABAGLIONE AND MASCARPONE INSERTS

176 g	**egg yolk**
230 g	**caster (superfine) sugar**
40 ml	**dark rum**
35 ml	**dry Marsala wine**
100 g	**fresh mascarpone cheese**

Make a zabaglione by whisking the egg yolk with the sugar, rum and wine over a bain-marie, then cool the hot mixture in a mixer by running on the lowest speed. Mix the cold zabaglione with the mascarpone until combined, then fill 2.5-cm-/1-inch-diameter spherical moulds. Melt the white chocolate and dilute it with the sunflower oil. Dip the zabaglione inserts into the chocolate and freeze. Put the spice-infused milk into a large pan and add the rice. Bring to the boil and cook for 16–17 minutes until the liquid is absorbed. Remove from the heat, add the mascarpone and stir until smooth. Allow to cool, then chill in the fridge. Take a portion of the chilled rice and mould it into a ball with your hands, then press a frozen zabaglione insert into the rice ball. Once all the balls have been formed, put them into the freezer again to firm. Dredge the firm balls in flour, then dip in beaten egg and roll in breadcrumbs to coat. Immediately before serving, preheat the oven to 180°C/350°F. Heat enough sunflower oil for deep-frying in a large, deep pan to 180°C/350°F, or until a cube of bread browns in 30 seconds. Carefully add the arancini balls to the hot oil and deep-fry until they are an even golden colour. Remove and drain on kitchen paper (paper towels), then bake in the oven for 4 minutes. Remove from the oven and allow to rest for 3–4 minutes, then sprinkle with icing (confectioners') sugar and serve hot, preferably on a bed of incandescent coarse salt scented with citrus fruits and Christmas spices.

Burnt chocolate and blanched parsley

Serves 6

12	**portions burnt milk bavarois** (see below)
50 g	**Parsley sauce** (see page 209)
12 g	**unblanched almonds**, roasted and salted
60 g	**parsley sorbet** (see below)
	lemon zest
	salted caramel (see below)
15 g	**blanched parsley**

FOR THE PARSLEY SORBET

550 g	**parsley leaves**
600 ml	**sparkling water**
150 g	**glucose syrup**
50 g	**almond syrup**
	salt

Blanch the parsley as for the sauce (see page 209). In a large pan, heat the sparkling water and glucose to 80°C/176°F and transfer to a blender. Add the parsley, almond syrup and a pinch of salt. Blend, strain and churn.

FOR THE CRÈME ANGLAISE

100 g	**egg yolk**
125 g	**condensed milk**, vacuum-sealed in a bag and steamed for 8 hours at 85°C/185°F
250 ml	**double (heavy) cream**
250 ml	**milk**

In a large heatproof bowl, whisk the egg yolk with the condensed milk. In a large pan, combine the cream and milk, bring to the boil and pour over the egg yolk mixture. Cook the crème anglaise until thick (82–84°C/180–183°F), then strain through a fine-mesh sieve (strainer).

FOR THE BURNT MILK BAVAROIS

3	**sheets isinglass**
350 g	**crème anglaise** (see above)
205 g	**blond (caramelized white) chocolate**, chopped
450 ml	**cold soft-whipped cream**
	melted dark chocolate, as needed
	activated charcoal, for dusting
	cocoa powder, as needed
	edible silver powder, for dusting

Soak the isinglass in plenty of cold water to rehydrate, then dissolve the isinglass in the freshly made crème anglaise. Add the mixture to the chopped blond (caramelized white) chocolate in a large bowl and stir with a wooden spoon until thick and smooth. When the mixture cools to 35–40°C/95–104°F, incorporate the cold soft-whipped cream. Fill single-portion moulds or square moulds for cutting into individual portions and spray. Spread the portions with dark chocolate, brush with activated charcoal and sprinkle with cocoa powder and silver powder.

FOR THE SALTED CARAMEL

200 ml	**double (heavy) cream**
30 g	**unsalted butter**
6 g	**Maldon sea salt**
120 g	**sugar**
90 g	**glucose syrup**

In a pan, heat the cream with the butter and sea salt. In a small pan, caramelize the sugar and glucose at 175°C/347°F. Stop the cooking process with the cream mixture, then return to the heat until the caramel has completely melted. Strain.

ASSEMBLY
Arrange bavarois portions on each serving plate and decorate with the parsley sauce, 2 salted almonds and a quenelle of parsley sorbet. Add some lemon zest, salted caramel and some blanched parsley leaves

Frozen fruit assortment

Serves 8

WATERMELON
For the apple jelly rind
400 g **Granny Smith apples**
1 litre **water**
1 g **ascorbic acid**
25 g **inverted sugar**
1,8 g **agar-agar**
8 g **isinglass**, rehydrated in cold water

150 g **white chocolate (33% cocoa solids)**
20 ml **vegetable oil**

To make the green apple juice, cut the Granny Smith apples into pieces and vacuum-seal in a bag with the water and ascorbic acid, removing as much air as possible. Once the citric acid has been absorbed by the fruit, pass the apple pieces through a juicer. In a pan, combine the 350 ml of the apple juice with the inverted sugar and bring to the boil. Add the agar-agar and bring back to the rehydrated boil while whisking briskly. Remove from the heat and add the isinglass. Quickly cool in a blast chiller, then refrigerate for 2 hours at 4°C/39°F to set. Whisk the mixture to a smooth and creamy consistency. Apply a vacuum to remove any air bubbles, then transfer to a piping (pastry) bag.

For the raspberry sorbet insert
435 ml **water**
100 g **glucose syrup**
1 kg **raspberry purée**
280 g **caster (superfine) sugar**
70 ml **lemon juice**
20 g **basil seeds**

To make the sorbet base, heat the water in a pan and dissolve the glucose. Transfer to a blender and gradually blend in the raspberry purée, sugar and lemon juice. Churn the sorbet base and incorporate the basil seeds to reproduce watermelon flesh and seeds.

Assembly
Melt the chocolate and incorporate the oil to make the mixture smooth and easier to work with. Line 6.5-cm-diameter silicone hemisphere moulds with a thin layer of the chocolate. Allow the chocolate to harden, then fill the moulds with the raspberry sorbet insert. Allow the hemispheres to harden in the freezer, then remove from the moulds and return to the freezer. Wash and carefully dry the moulds. Put a tablespoon of apple jelly into each mould and add a frozen insert, pressing until the jelly is about to leak out from around it. Freeze for 2 hours. Remove the hemispheres from their moulds and slice into wedges to make mock watermelon slices.

PASSION FRUIT
For the rind
300 ml **blueberry juice**
1,8 g **agar-agar**
1 **sheet isinglass**, rehydrated in cold water

In a pan, combine the blueberry juice with the agar-agar and bring to the boil. Add the rehydrated isinglass and allow to dissolve. Quickly cool in a blast chiller, then refrigerate the mixture for 2 hours. Blend until smooth and creamy and apply a vacuum to remove any air bubbles.

For the milk ice cream intermediate layer
180 g **caster (superfine) sugar**
20 g **dextrose**
25 g **milk powder**
1 litre **fresh milk**
80 ml **double (heavy) cream**

Mix the sugar, dextrose and milk powder together. In a pan, heat the fresh milk to 50°C/122°F, add the sugar mixture and bring to 80°C/176°F. Add the cream and increase the temperature to 88°C/190°F. Quickly cool to 4°C/39°F in a blast chiller and churn the ice cream.

For the mango sorbet insert
870 ml **water**
280 g **caster (superfine) sugar**
100 g **glucose syrup**
1 kg **mango purée**
70 ml **lemon juice**

In a large pan, heat the water, sugar and glucose to 80°C/176°F. Allow to cool, then mix with the mango purée and lemon juice. Refrigerate the sorbet base overnight, then churn the sorbet the next day.

Assembly
Fill 1.5-cm-/⅝-inch-diameter hemisphere moulds with the mango sorbet insert and freeze. Fill a 4-cm-/1½-inch-diameter hemisphere mould three-quarters full with the milk ice cream intermediate layer. Press a mango sorbet insert into the centre and freeze. Remove the frozen hemispheres from the moulds. Wash the moulds, add 1 heaped tablespoon of blueberry jelly (rind) and press the ice cream and mango hemisphere into them and freeze. Remove the mock passion fruit halves from the moulds and neaten with a small knife.

COCONUT
For the chocolate jelly shell
300 ml **milk**
40 g **glucose syrup**
3 g **agar-agar**
70 g **dark chocolate** (72% cocoa solids), chopped
30 g **blond chocolate** (35% cocoa solids), chopped

In a pan, bring the milk, glucose and agar-agar to the boil. Add the hot mixture to the chopped chocolates in a heatproof bowl and whisk until smooth. Allow to cool and set, then blend to a creamy gel.

For the coconut ice cream insert
180 g **caster (superfine) sugar**
20 g **dextrose**
25 g **milk powder**
100 g **coconut flour**
1 litre **fresh milk**
80 ml **double (heavy) cream**

Mix the sugar, dextrose, milk powder and coconut flour together in a bowl. In a large pan, heat the fresh milk to 50°C/122°F, add the sugar mixture and bring to 80°C/176°F. Add the cream and increase the temperature to 88°C/190°F. Quickly cool to 4°C/39°F and churn the ice cream. Line an oval mould with a rounded base with the ice cream and freeze until the moulded shell can be easily removed.

Assembly
Line the same mould with foil. Spread a layer of chocolate jelly and press in the coconut ice cream insert. Freeze. Remove the mock coconut from the mould and break up into irregular pieces.

TO SERVE
Serve the frozen fruit on a bed of ice, alternating the watermelon slices with broken coconut pieces and freshly made passion fruit halves topped with a teaspoon of fresh pulp.

Chocolate and lardo soufflés

Makes 10 soufflés

CHOCOLATE SOUFFLÉS

butter, for greasing
80 g **caster (superfine) sugar**, plus extra for sprinkling
300 g **Papua New Guinea dark chocolate** (at least 70% cocoa solids), chopped
300 ml **fresh milk**
20 g **cornflour (cornstarch)**
4 **drops Tabasco sauce**
1,5 g **chilli powder**
1 g **Maldon sea salt**
60 g **egg yolk**
200 g **egg white**
10 **thin slices aged lardo (cured pork back fat) with mugwort**

Grease the soufflé dishes with butter and sprinkle with sugar. Set aside. Melt the chocolate in a large heatproof bowl. Whisk 50 g of the cold milk with the cornflour (cornstarch), taking care to prevent lumps forming. Add it to the remaining milk, with the Tabasco, chilli powder, and salt in a pan and bring to the boil. Add the hot milk to the melted chocolate and whisk until smooth. When the chocolate mixture is at 50°C/122°F, incorporate the egg yolk. At the same time, beat the egg white and the 80 g sugar to stiff peaks. Add a little of the beaten egg white to the first mixture and mix gently with a silicone spatula until smooth, then fold in the remaining egg white. Fill the prepared soufflé dishes to the top with the batter, then smooth the tops well with a spatula and wipe any batter off the rim with your fingers. Bake in a static oven at 200°C/400°F for 9–10 minutes.

FOR THE BANANA AND HORSERADISH SAUCE

2 **ripe bananas**
200 ml **water**
20 g **fresh horseradish juice**

Blend the bananas with the water and horseradish juice on high speed. Strain and set aside in the fridge until ready to serve.

ASSEMBLY

Top the freshly baked soufflés topped with 2 half-slices of lardo and serve. At the table, use a serving spoon to break open the soufflé top, as is traditional, and pour a tablespoon of the banana and horseradish sauce into the opening.

Gold bars and silver nuggets

Makes 25–30 shortbreads

FOR THE BLACK SHORTBREAD

75 g **Caraïbe dark chocolate** (at least 66% cocoa solids)
135 g **soft wheat flour** (W index 180–230)
18 g **cocoa powder**
4 g **bicarbonate of soda (baking soda)**
40 g **icing (confectioners') sugar**
75 g **light brown sugar**
115 g **unsalted butter**, softened
1,7 g **Maldon sea salt**
8 g **ground coffee powder**
gold food colouring, for spraying

Chill the chocolate in the fridge, then grind it to fine crumbs. Sift the flour, cocoa, bicarbonate of soda (baking soda) and sugars into a mixer fitted with the paddle attachment. Incorporate the softened butter and mix to form a dough. Finally, mix in the ground chocolate, salt and coffee powder. Fill the specific moulds with the shortbread and bake at 180°C/350°F for 20 minutes, then 6–8 minutes at 150°C/302°F. Allow to cool, then spray with gold food colouring.

FOR THE WHITE SHORTBREAD

90 g **unsalted butter**, softened
90 g **caster (superfine) sugar**
48 g **soft wheat flour** (W index 180–230)
45 g **ground almonds**
38 g **egg**
148 g **soft wheat flour** (W index 180–230)
1,2 g **salt**
45 g **white chocolate**, melted
silver food colouring, for spraying

In a mixer fitted with a paddle attachment, mix the butter with the sugar, the 48 g flour and the ground almonds on low speed. When combined, add the egg, then incorporate the 148 g flour and salt without allowing the resulting dough to develop structure. Roll the dough out between 2 sheets of baking (parchment) paper until 6–7 mm/⅙–¼ inch thick and bake at 155°C/311°F for 28–30 minutes. The shortbread should be cooked through while retaining its light colour. Allow the pastry to cool, then grind to crumbs in a blender. Combine the crumbs with the melted white chocolate to make a new shortbread. Use your fingers to shape the shortbread into nuggets and arrange them spaced apart on a baking tray. Spray them with the white mixture and then with silver food colouring.

Dark chocolate and dried olives

Serves 10–12

FOR THE DARK CHOCOLATE GANACHE

150 ml **double (heavy) cream**
15 g **glucose powder**
5 g **dried olive powder**, plus extra for sprinkling
0.5 g **fresh thyme**, plus extra to decorate
250 g **dark chocolate** (at least 70% cocoa solids), chopped
0.5 g **Maldon sea salt**

In a large pan, heat the cream and glucose powder to 80°C/176°F, then add the olive powder and fresh thyme. Allow to steep for 3–4 minutes, then strain into a clean pan. Bring the infused cream to the boil and add to the chocolate and salt in a large heatproof bowl. Whisk to a smooth, creamy consistency. Fill spherical moulds and allow to set. Remove the balls from the moulds, place in a presentation spoon and finish with dried olive powder and a fresh thyme leaf.

Barbajada

Serves 6

45 g **bitter cocoa powder**
15 g **ground coffee**
60 ml **double (heavy) cream**
140 ml **water**
160 g **glucose syrup**
2 **sheets isinglass**, rehydrated in cold water
100 ml **soft-whipped cream**, to serve

In a large bowl, mix the cocoa, coffee and cream together. Make a syrup with the water and the glucose, then while still hot, add it to the cocoa and cream mixture and whisk until the cocoa and coffee are completely dissolved. Add the rehydrated isinglass and refrigerate.

ASSEMBLY

Immediately before serving, briskly whisk the mixture until lightly frothy, then pour into a serving glass and top with ½ tablespoon of soft-whipped cream.

Tomato and ginger

White fish

Fish and saffron

Smoked blueberry gel

Sweet-and-sour mushroom

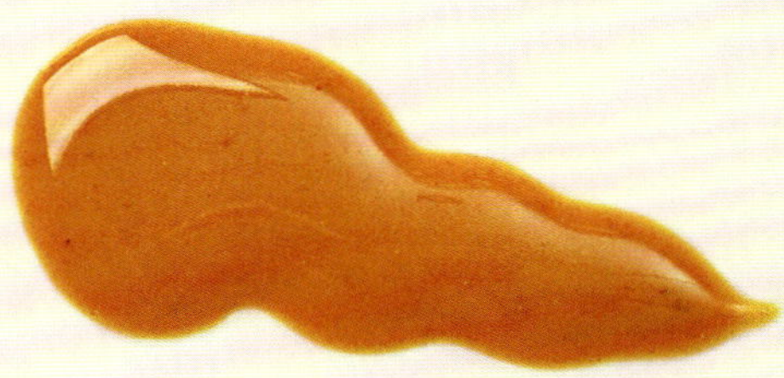

Pink pickling liquor gel

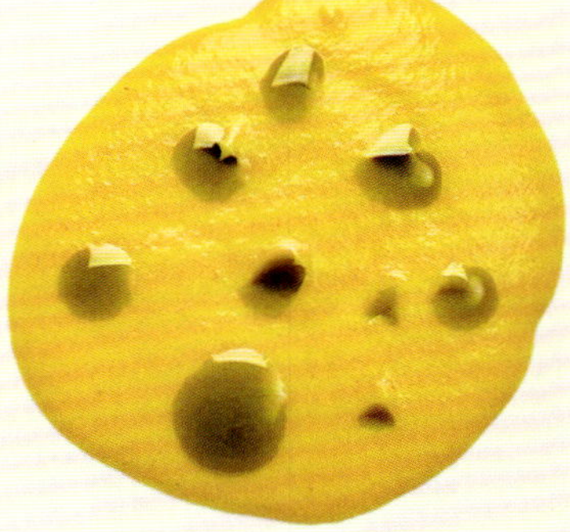

Yellow pepper, cumin and coriander

Roasted pine nut paste

Parsley
Raw tomato
Smoked scamorza gel
Pickling liquor and soy sauce gel
Sweet-and-sour pepper, ginger and spice
Sweet-and-sour carrot
Romesco
Italiana
Black almond and truffle

SAUCES

TOMATO AND GINGER SAUCE

for meat and fish salads, rice dishes and stews

90 g **fresh ginger**, peeled
½ **white onion**, julienned
1 **clove garlic**, chopped
15 g **extra-virgin olive oil**
500 g **passata (sieved tomatoes)**
salt

Push the ginger through a juicer and set the juice aside (discard solids). In a pan, sauté the onion and garlic in the olive oil until soft. Add the passata (sieved tomatoes) and simmer for 30 minutes. The sauce should thicken without losing too much volume. Adjust the seasoning with salt and blend in the fresh ginger juice to a thick, creamy and intensely flavoured sauce.

WHITE FISH

to serve with Char in a pastry crust (see page 252)

100 g **leek**, chopped
100 g **celery**, chopped
100 g **onion**, chopped
1 **clove garlic**, chopped
1 **bay leaf**
extra-virgin olive oil, for cooking
1 litre **Barbecued white fish stock** (see page 252)
white wine vinegar, as needed
salt and ground white pepper

In a pan, sauté all the vegetables and the bay leaf in the olive oil until soft. Cover with the stock and cook gently until it is reduced by a third. Remove and discard the bay leaf and blend everything together. Adjust the seasoning with vinegar, salt and white pepper. It can also be enriched with chopped herbs, such as chives, chervil, tarragon and mint, if you like.

FISH AND SAFFRON

for fish steaks that are poached or roasted with their skin

1 litre Barbecued white fish stock (see page 252)
100 g **leek**, chopped
100 g **celery**, chopped
100 g **onion**, chopped
200 g **fennel**, chopped
1 **clove garlic**
1 **bay leaf**
extra-virgin olive oil, for cooking
2 g **fennel seeds**
1/3 **liquorice root**
0.3 g **saffron threads**
white wine vinegar, as needed
salt and ground white pepper

Proceed as for the basic white fish sauce (see above) but add the saffron after using an immersion blender and allow it to steep in the sauce for 15 minutes before whisking until smooth. The saffron threads can also be blended for a smoother sauce.

PARSLEY

for the Burnt milk bavarois (see page 211)

200 g **parsley leaves**
300 ml **sparkling water**
20 g **glucose syrup**
110 g **almond syrup**

Blanch the parsley in a pan of boiling water for 5 minutes, then refresh in a bowl of iced water. Drain and blend with the sparkling water, glucose and almond syrup until smooth and consistent. Strain through a fine-mesh sieve (strainer).

RAW TOMATO SAUCE

for the Warm spaghetti with a barbecued fish, tomato and ginger sauce (see page 205)

400 g **very ripe datterini tomatoes**, halved
5 g **caster (superfine) sugar**
1 **clove garlic** (unpeeled)
10 **basil leaves**, chopped
extra-virgin olive oil, if needed

Put the tomatoes into a large bowl with the sugar, unpeeled garlic clove and chopped basil leaves. Allow to marinate for 2 hours, then remove and discard the garlic and basil leaves. Blend and press through a fine-mesh sieve (strainer) into a smooth, creamy and flavourful sauce.

SMOKED BLUEBERRY GEL

for game and cheese dishes

3 **sprigs rosemary**
1 kg **fresh blueberries**
300 ml **water**
20 g **caster (superfine) sugar**
2 g **ground white pepper**
20 ml **balsamic vinegar**
5 ml **red shallot vinegar**
agar-agar, as needed

Burn the rosemary with a flame, then add it to a large jar with an airtight lid with the blueberries. Seal the jar and let the smoke from the burning rosemary accumulate inside. Meanwhile, bring the water, sugar and white pepper to the boil in a large pan. Add the smoked blueberries and whisk until smooth. Add the balsamic and shallot vinegars and bring to the boil. Add 0.9 g of agar-agar for every 100 g of the liquid and dissolve. Allow to cool and set, then purée in a blender to a smooth gel. Apply a vacuum several times to remove any air bubbles.

SWEET-AND-SOUR MUSHROOMS

to add strong and fragrant sweet-and-sour notes

1 **shallot**, chopped
1 **clove garlic**, chopped
extra-virgin olive oil, for cooking
1 kg **assorted mushrooms (porcini, chanterelle and white mushrooms)**, chopped
200 ml **apple cider vinegar**
125 g **light brown sugar**
10 g **salt**
10 g **soy sauce**
200 g **fresh vine tomatoes**
10 g **tomato purée (paste)**
10 g **black peppercorns**
2 **teaspoons wholegrain mustard**
1 **bay leaf**
1 **whole clove**

In a pan, sauté the shallot and garlic in the olive oil until soft. Add the mushrooms and sauté until coloured. Deglaze with the vinegar and add the remaining ingredients. Cover with a lid and cook for 20 minutes. Uncover and continue to simmer to cook off the liquid for about 10 minutes. Remove from the heat and cool quickly, then vacuum-seal in a bag and refrigerate for 20 days. After this time, transfer the contents of the bag to a blender and purée until it is a thick, velvety and creamy sauce, rich in flavour and aromas.

PICKLING LIQUOR AND SOY SAUCE GEL

to accompany deep-fried fish

125 ml **white wine**
90 g **white onion**
75 ml **apple cider vinegar**
50 ml **white vinegar**
25 g **acacia honey**
10 ml **rice wine vinegar**
5 g **ground white pepper**
1 **bay leaf**
1 **sage leaf**
200 ml **water**
agar-agar, as needed
soy sauce, as needed

In a large pan, combine all ingredients, except the agar-agar and soy sauce, with the water and bring to the boil. Cover, turn off the heat and allow to steep for 10 minutes. Strain and weigh the resulting liquid. Add 1 g agar-agar for every 100 g of pickling liquor. Allow to set in the fridge, then blend to a soft and smooth gel. Using a syringe, inject a drop of soy sauce into the centre of the sauce.

SMOKED SCAMORZA GEL

for the Aubergine carpaccio alla Norma (see page 203)

200 ml **water**
125 ml **fresh milk**
175 g **smoked scamorza cheese**, cut into pieces
salt and ground black pepper
agar-agar, as needed

In a large pan, heat the water and the milk together to 60°C/140°F. Transfer to a Thermomix and add the cheese. Run the Thermomix on medium speed and set the temperature to 55°C/131°F, then blend on the highest speed setting. Once the temperature has been reached, strain the liquid through a sieve (strainer) and season with salt and pepper. Add 0.8 g of agar-agar for every 100 g of liquid and dissolve. Allow to cool and set in the fridge. Cut the jelly into pieces and blend to a smooth gel.

SWEET-AND-SOUR PEPPER, GINGER AND SPICE SAUCE

for braised meat or fish

2 **tablespoons extra-virgin olive oil**
1 **white onion, chopped**
2 **red (bell) peppers**, peeled, de-seeded and cut into small pieces
100 g **light brown sugar**
100 ml **apple cider vinegar**
1 **tablespoon grated peeled fresh ginger**
1 g **ground turmeric**
1 g **ground cinnamon**
1 g **fresh chilli**, chopped
salt

Heat the olive oil in a large pan and sauté the chopped onion until soft. Add the (bell) peppers, cover with a lid and cook over a low heat for 10 minutes. Add the sugar and vinegar, reduce the heat to very low and cook for a further 20 minutes. Add the spices and chilli and adjust the seasoning with salt. Blend until it is a thick, translucent and luscious sauce.

PINK PICKLING LIQUOR GEL

for the Lombard-style frog soup and frog croquettes (see page 199) or to accompany deep-fried or crispy fish

125 ml **white wine**
90 g **Tropea red onion**, finely diced
75 ml **raspberry vinegar**
50 ml **white vinegar**
25 g **acacia honey**
10 ml **red shallot vinegar**
5 g **ground white pepper**
1 **bay leaf**
1 **sage leaf**
200 ml **water**
agar-agar, as needed

Bring all the ingredients, except the agar-agar, with the water to the boil in a large pan. Cover with a lid, turn off the heat and allow to steep for 10 minutes. Strain and weigh the resulting liquid. Add 1 g agar-agar for every 100 g of pickling liquor. Allow to set in the fridge, then purée in a blender to a soft and smooth gel.

ROMESCO

for fish and roasted vegetables

250 g **red (bell) pepper**, charred and peeled
150 g **very ripe vine tomatoes**
80 g **unblanched almonds**
80 g **blanched almonds**
20 g **crusco chillies**
20 ml **red wine vinegar**
70 ml **extra-virgin olive oil**
50 ml **olive oil**
10 g **basil leaves**
10 g **parsley leaves**
5 g **garlic**
5 g **smoked paprika**
5 g **salt**
½ **red chilli**
60 ml **water**
juice and zest of 1 lemon

Purée all the ingredients with the water in a blender to a rich, smooth and full-bodied sauce.

SWEET-AND-SOUR CARROT SAUCE

to season bitter and crunchy vegetables

450 g **carrots**, sliced
2 **tablespoons extra-virgin olive oil**
25 g **light brown sugar**
5 g **salt**
3 **juniper berries**
3 **whole cloves**
1 **cinnamon stick**
1 **bay leaf**
1 **clove garlic**
100 ml **white wine vinegar**

In a large pan, sauté the sliced carrots in the olive oil until tender. Add the sugar, salt, spices, bay leaf and garlic and deglaze with the vinegar. Cover with a lid and cook for 30 minutes over a low heat. Uncover and finish cooking. Cool quickly and vacuum-seal in a bag. Refrigerate for 20 days, then transfer the contents of the bag to a blender and purée to a rich and spicy sauce.

YELLOW PEPPER, CUMIN AND CORIANDER SAUCE

to season poached round fish and rice

2 **white onions**, chopped
3 **yellow (bell) peppers**, peeled, de-seeded and chopped
80 ml **white rice vinegar**
15 g **coriander seeds**
2 g **cumin**
salt
50 g **basil leaves**
20 g **coriander (cilantro) leaves**

Sauté the onions in a pan until soft. Add the peppers and sauté until coloured. Deglaze with the vinegar, then add the spices and bring to the boil. Adjust the seasoning with salt, then purée in a blender with the basil leaves and coriander (cilantro).

TOASTED PINE NUT PASTE

to finish for the dish Love in Portofino (see page 202)

200 g **pine nuts**, toasted and still warm
200 g **sunflower oil**
1 g **ground white pepper**
1 g **salt**

Blend the still-warm pine nuts with the remaining ingredients to a thick and smooth paste.

ITALIANA

for roasted meat

2,5 kg **veal trimmings**
5 kg **veal rib bones**
1 **bunch spring onions (scallions)**
1 **celery stick (stalk)**
½ **bulb garlic**
10 **red onions**
1 **red chilli**
2 **bay leaves**
2 **sprigs rosemary**
5 **sprigs thyme**
4 kg **Piccadilly tomatoes**, halved
300 g **basil leaves**
5 kg **ice cubes**
5 litres **beef stock**
150 g **tomato purée (paste)**

Brown the meat and remove the fat. Roast the bones in the oven at 200°C/400°F until completely browned. In a large, high-sided pan, sauté the spring onions (scallions), celery, garlic, red onions, red chilli, bay leaves, rosemary and thyme until coloured. Add the veal trimmings and bones, halved tomatoes and enough basil and ice to cover the contents of the pan. Add the stock and slowly bring to the boil. Skim off the scum constantly and simmer for about 3 hours. Add the remaining ice and continue to cook for a further 2 hours. Add the remaining basil and allow to steep for 20 minutes. Strain and reduce to thick, glossy, refreshing and flavourful sauce.

BLACK ALMONDS AND TRUFFLE SAUCE

for pan-fried seafood

250 g **blanched almonds**
20 g **squid ink**
20 g **black truffle paste**
15 ml **red shallot vinegar**
10 ml **extra-virgin olive oil**
5 g **salt**
2 **cloves black garlic**
0.2 g **xanthan gum**
600 ml **water**

Soak the almonds in a large bowl of water overnight. The next day, transfer the almonds to a blender with the remaining ingredients and blend until smooth and creamy.

SALA MENGONI

In the Sala Mengoni, we summon up the noblest sweet and savoury recipes of classic cuisine, but we strive to imbue them with new light and with a different kind of dignity and quality that is accessible to all, both in taste and style of presentation.

The second floor at Cracco in Galleria is the only one that can be accessed via a secondary entrance, the lift (elevator) on Via Silvio Pellico, which crosses the Galleria's cruciform plan. The lift takes you to Sala Mengoni, which is of course named after the architect who conceived the whole Salotto di Milano. More recent architects have tried to transfer the textures of Mengoni's late nineteenth-century iron latticework to the interior, which dazzles with all its charm when viewed from the iron balconies on which professional photographers and Instagrammers happily climb: they know full well that the view from the top of the Octagon over the Galleria has few equals.
Inside Sala Mengoni, the row of pillars supporting the entablatures is very striking. Just like the Galleria, it makes guests feel that they are at the centre of a special space. The ceiling is painted with original late nineteenth-century frescoes, while the adaptability of the furnishings, including a large levanto marble counter from the 1920s, helps to create a magnificent and versatile space.

Sala Mengoni is a venue for a whole variety of events of different sizes: it can accommodate anything from a private table for two to occasions involving up to a hundred standing guests. The menu in the Sala, which is always bespoke to the customer, focuses on a range of cuisine that differ from Cracco's other venues, because we strongly believe that each level of the building should have its own distinct personality. In the Sala Mengoni we take our time to

reproduce the meticulous aristocratic menus of Italian, French or Bourbon-era gastronomy, including 'sformati', 'timballi' and many other fascinating specialities that have evolved to perfection over the decades. These are complex and opulent dishes, whether sweet, savoury or both. The menu hints at the royal courts, as does the visual spectacle of the venue, with architecture dazzling both inside and outside the stained-glass windows.

Seafood cocktail with marinated egg yolk sauce and Crodino

SEAFOOD COCKTAIL WITH MARINATED EGG YOLK SAUCE AND CRODINO

In Italy, the langoustine or prawn (shrimp) cocktail is a dish that transcends the generations. Virtually everyone knows it, and the popular imagination tends to associate it with the 1980s. In fact, the custom of combining boiled shellfish with a cocktail sauce began in the United States in Prohibition times, during the 1920s, when the cocktails were deliberately served in martini or daiquiri glasses so as to provide cover for the possession of glasses that were illegal to fill with alcohol. We know for sure that the recipe was popular across the Atlantic in the 1950s, where the Golden Gate Hotel in Las Vegas served it with cooked prawns on the rim, and this dish was so successful that the hotel celebrated the sale of its 25 millionth cocktail in 2007. Since the 1960s, the seafood cocktail has known endless variations, from Spain to Mexico, and from Great Britain to Italy.

At the restaurant, we prepare it in a contemporary style: our langoustines, lobsters and prawns have a good bite because they are freshly boiled (and not overcooked, as is traditionally the case). We transformed the traditional cocktail sauce by combining a paste of marinated egg yolk *(see page 250)* with small portions of tomato. This expedient adds extra savour and a fullness of flavour. We also add a touch of shellfish bisque, taking care with the proportions to reach a balanced ratio of sauce to shellfish. Alongside these two key ingredients, we place a hyper-crunchy lettuce heart and a reduced Crodino bitters jelly, carefully selecting the botanicals that distinguish this aperitif (nutmeg, cardamom, carnation...). Then we add more caper powder, green apple and raw celery to restore the acidity missing because of the lack of the traditional lemon. We serve the cocktail in an old-fashioned champagne coupe, with a slightly larger diameter.

TIMBALE IN THE GALLERIA

'The burnished gold of the crusts, the fragrance of the sugar and cinnamon they exuded, were but preludes to the delights bursting forth from the interior when the knife broke through the crust. First came a smoke suffused with aromas, then chicken livers, hard-boiled eggs, sliced ham, chicken, and truffles in heaps of piping hot glistening macaroni, to which the meat added an exquisite hue of suede.'

This is one of the most fascinating dishes ever to be described. The evocative words belong to the Sicilian writer Giuseppe Tomasi di Lampedusa, put into the mouth of his great-grandfather Giulio Fabrizio Tomasi, the protagonist of *The Leopard* (1958). This was the first Italian novel to sell hundreds of thousands of copies worldwide, and director Luchino Visconti transformed it into an equally famous film with a stellar cast (Claudia Cardinale, Alain Delon, Burt Lancaster...). Di Lampedusa's quote describes the dish known as 'timballo di maccheroni', which of course later became known as 'timballo del Gattopardo', a fascinating recipe that takes us back once again to the so-called 'monsù cuisine', originally produced by the cooks of the aristocratic Bourbon courts.

In the restaurant we grew up with the myth of di Lampedusa's sumptuous words, so much so that we could recite them by heart. We have worked long and hard to replicate even a hint of those sensations in our diners' taste buds. Everyone deserves to experience that extravagant recipe updated to the times in which we live. Starting with the crust, we decided to do away with the original shortcrust pastry, which was too sweet and thick. Instead, we prepared an eggless, thinner, lighter and savoury brisée pastry, flavouring it with cinnamon. We semi-salted the cream, and transformed it into a Milanese-style sauce, using saffron, shallots and Parmigiano; for the filling, we cooked a ragout of kidney with Marsala and black truffle, accompanied by many staples of the original recipe: peas, hard-boiled eggs, calf's liver and chicken breasts. At the base of the preparation is a layer of rigatoni mantecati. We put the pie crust over the filling, bake everything in the oven and cut into the pie at the table itself, while reciting Tomasi di Lampedusa's description. The diners gasp.

Timbale in the Galleria

Seafood cocktail with marinated egg yolk sauce and Crodino

Timbale Flammand

TIMBALE FLAMMAND

Also known as 'bucatini cerino', timbale flammand is one of the most fascinating dishes of the Bourbon era. In the second half of the eighteenth century, the kitchens of Ferdinand IV were ruled by the 'monsù', industrious cooks who loved to interweave the aristocratic traditions of southern Italy with the most elaborate French techniques. This timbale was a flan, or 'sformato', made from bucatini. It was called 'flammand' not only because of its alleged Flemish origins, but also because it was served at the table with a burning flame from a wick, often inserted into an eggshell filled with alcohol and lit at the time of serving. Such a flamboyant presentation gave added charm to this dome of bucatini, enclosing a swirl of opulent ingredients.

We have tried to respect the aristocratic magnificence of this dish, only with our own twist. The spiral of pasta is smeared underneath with a cream of chicken and black truffle, then topped with a thin layer of saffron-flavoured rice mantecato, and, after that, a rich filling of meatballs, tomatoes, boiled eggs, peas and mushrooms. The half sphere is covered, baked and served with the flaming wick – this always generates widespread 'oohs' and 'ahs' in the room. It is a more domestic timbale, with a contemporary freshness, but nevertheless just as breathtaking as it was in the time of the Bourbons.

Bejewelled quail

BEJEWELLED QUAIL

The story of this dish is a journey that begins far away, in both space and time. The starting point was the 'jewelled rice' of the Jewish-Persian tradition, a dish that was prepared in advance, then reheated or eaten cold on the days of Shabbat, the day of rest. In essence, it is a colourful basmati, cooked in turmeric and coriander, very multihued and joyful to the eye. Because we are conscious of our regional specialities, we decided to adapt this recipe to a bird from our traditions: the quail. Its stuffing is a classic saffron rice with a very distinct acidity, embellished with dried apricots, sultanas (golden raisins) soaked in white wine and a little cheese and spices (coriander berries and leaves, cumin, pink pepper and chives). We spruce up the quail with torn coriander (cilantro) leaves and flower petals, placing next to it a spinach and anise cream to enhance the overall spiciness. This dish may take us on an exotic journey, but at the same time we find ourselves even closer to home than we might have imagined: quail and rice, what could be more Lombardian than that?

CHAR IN A PASTRY CRUST

Of all the magnificent recipes for pastry-crusted fish in the noblest classical cuisines, it is perhaps the salmon coulibiac that has always truly captured our imagination. Already, in the early twentieth century, Georges August Escoffier, the father of haute cuisine, was singing the praises of this recipe for salmon in a puff pastry or brioche crust, originally deriving from Russia and Eastern Europe. In its many variations, coulibiac could be stuffed with boiled eggs, mushrooms, onions, spinach, rice or buckwheat. In our take on this dish, instead of salmon, we use the heart of a fillet of Trentino char, enriching it with pumpkin and mustard, in a filling that we find very tasty. Portioning it out in front of the diners is an essential part of the festive ceremony. This is a hard-working speciality that brings the whole table to life.

Char in a pastry crust

PANETTONE ALLA MILANESE

Our city is the birthplace of the world's best-selling cake. We call it not just panettone but 'panettone alla Milanese', because any recipe that becomes truly international over time inevitably takes on many alternative forms, some very different from the original. For us, panettone (which derives from *pan de ton*, meaning 'luxury bread') must consist of a soft, rich bread, made with a healthy percentage of fat, like the delicious panettone that the Besuschio pastry shop in Abbiategrasso, the birthplace of our chef Luca Sacchi, has been producing for generations.
The preparation of panettone is generally a laborious process, and even more so with ours, as we are very careful to select only the highest quality ingredients, such as sun-kissed Zibibbo sultanas (golden raisins), organic and certified. Crispy and fragrant, the Cracco panettone is soft and easy to munch, giving diners maximum satisfaction. We are very happy to prepare it eight metres (26 feet) above the Café della Galleria; just like any village shop.

TIRAMISU PROFITEROLES

The illustrious prototype for this recipe was Marie-Antoine Carême's 'croquembouche', a pyramid of custard or chantilly cream puffs, doused with a golden caramel sauce, which this pioneer of French 'grande cuisine' created in the early nineteenth century. Like Carême's original, our profiteroles are a generous *pièce montée* (decorative confectionery centrepiece), a hymn both to festivity and to the joyful sharing of food. They are a veritable mountain of Italian-style cream puffs: the choux buns are filled with coffee cream and mascarpone, enhanced with crunchy caramel and bitter cocoa. Not only is this a dish worthy of the table of Louis XVI, but it also generates powerful emotions in those who taste it.

Panettone alla Milanese

RECIPES
FROM THE SALA MENGONI

Seafood cocktail with marinated egg yolk sauce and Crodino

Serves 6

2	**steamed lobster tails**, cut into chunks
6	**steamed langoustine tails**, cut into chunks
6	**shrimp tails**, cut into chunks
250 g	**marinated yolk cocktail sauce** (see below)
60 g	**celery sticks, finely diced**
2 g	**torn celery leaves**
6	**caperberries in oil**
6	**non-alcoholic bitters jelly discs** (see below)

FOR THE MARINATED EGG YOLK COCKTAIL SAUCE

90 g	**marinated egg yolk**
90 g	**seafood stock reduction**
20 g	**tomato purée (paste)**
8 ml	**Cognac**
3 ml	**Worcestershire sauce**
3 ml	**vinegar**
1 g	**Tabasco sauce**
90 g	**sunflower oil**

Combine all the ingredients, except the oil, in a mixing beaker and blend until smooth and fluffy. Gradually emulsify with the oil until the sauce is thick, smooth, rich and creamy. Set side.

FOR THE NON-ALCOHOLIC BITTERS JELLY SAUCE

300 ml	**non-alcoholic bitters**
4	**whole cloves**
4	**cardamom pods**
16	**toasted coriander seeds**
8	**blades mace**
	zest of ½ pink grapefruit
3 g	**agar-agar**

In a pan, heat the bitters to 90°C/194°F, then add the remaining ingredients, except the agar-agar, and allow to steep for 10 minutes. Strain the liquid into a pan, bring to the boil and add 1 g agar agar for every 100 g of liquid. Spread the liquid over a plate to form a 2-mm-/1⁄16-inch-thick layer and allow to cool and set. Cut out thin, transparent discs of 6 cm/2½ inches in diameter with a round pastry cutter.

ASSEMBLY
Mix the seafood with the cocktail sauce. Add the diced celery and mix to combine, then place in desired serving glasses. Garnish the top with torn celery leaves and caperberry slices. Cover with a jelly disc veil and serve.

Timbale in the Galleria

Serves 6

½	**poached skinless chicken breast**
30 g	**egg**
80 g	**grated Parmigiano Reggiano cheese**
	butter, for frying
100 g	**fresh mushrooms**
100 g	**chicken livers**
60 g	**petits pois**, boiled to al dente
100 g	**cooked ham**, cut into small strips
80 g	**truffle**, cut into matchsticks (pregiato)
100 ml	**dry Marsala wine**
250 g	**rigatoni**, cooked
200 g	**veal kidney ragù**
200 g	**sugo di carne (meat sauce)**
	salt and ground black pepper

Mince (grind) the chicken meat, then mix with the egg and Parmesan and season with salt and pepper. Shape into meatballs the size of hazelnuts. In a large frying pan or skillet, fry the meatballs in butter until golden, then remove and pat dry with kitchen paper (paper towels). Add the mushrooms to the pan with the chicken livers, peas, ham and truffle and sauté, then deglaze with the Marsala. Adjust the seasoning with salt and pepper. Mix the rigatoni with the kidney ragù, chicken liver mixture and the meat sauce, stirring well to combine. Set aside.

FOR THE CINNAMON SHORTCRUST PASTRY

30 g	**ground cinnamon**
600 g	**soft wheat flour** (W index 180–230)
290 g	**cornflour (cornstarch)**
24 g	**salt**
7 g	**caster (superfine) sugar**
500 g	**unsalted butter**, softened
85 g	**egg**
17 ml	**white wine vinegar**
150 ml	**water**

In a large bowl, mix the cinnamon with the cornflour (cornstarch), salt and sugar. Rub the butter into the flour mixture. Add the egg and mix to combine, then incorporate the vinegar mixed with the water. Knead quickly and allow to rest in the fridge overnight.

FOR THE BLACK SHORTCRUST PASTRY

17 g	**squid ink**
72 ml	**water**
9 ml	**white wine vinegar**
290 g	**soft wheat flour** (W index 180–230)
145 g	**cornflour (cornstarch)**
9 g	**salt**
4 g	**caster (superfine) sugar**
250 g	**unsalted butter**, softened
25 g	**egg**

Mix the squid ink with the water and the vinegar, then proceed to make this pastry as for the cinnamon shortcrust pastry. Allow to rest in the fridge overnight.

FOR THE SAFFRON PASTRY CREAM

500 ml	**fresh milk**
80 g	**caster (superfine) sugar**
60 g	**soft wheat flour** (W index 180–230)
66 g	**egg yolk**
0.5 g	**saffron threads**
	salt and ground black pepper

Make a pastry cream with all the ingredients and set aside in the fridge.

ASSEMBLY

2	**hard-boiled eggs**, sliced
	saffron pastry cream (see above)

Preheat the oven to 180°C/350°F. Line a cake tin (pan) with the cinnamon pastry, leaving an overhang around the edges, then fill the pastry case to three-quarters with the rigatoni and sauce. Spread the slices of hard-boiled egg over the top and cover with a layer of saffron pastry cream. Cover the top with a disc of cinnamon pastry and decorate with a lattice of black pastry. Seal the edges and bake for 40 minutes. Remove from the oven and allow the pie to rest for 20 minutes, then remove it from the cake tin and serve. We like to accompany it with a vegetable sauce so as not to accentuate the meatiness and protein in the pie.

Timbale Flammand

Serves 6-8

	butter, for greasing
375 g	**large bucatini pasta**, cooked in salted water
250 g	**Creamy Saffron Rice filling** (see right)
	truffle shavings, to serve

FOR THE CHICKEN FORCEMEAT

350 g	**skinless, boneless chicken breast**
250 g	**cold béchamel sauce** (100 g white roux for 500 ml milk)
5 g	**grated Parmigiano Reggiano cheese**
44 g	**egg yolk**
	grated nutmeg, as needed
	salt and ground black pepper

Finely chop the chicken breast and mix with the cold béchamel sauce, Parmesan and egg yolk. Season with salt and pepper and nutmeg.

FOR THE FILLING

100 g	**coarsely minced (ground) veal** (assorted cuts) **and ½ chicken breast**
1	**tablespoon grated Parmigiano Reggiano cheese**
60 g	**egg**
	plain (all-purpose) flour, for dusting
	butter, for frying
200 g	**white mushrooms**
200 ml	**dry Marsala wine**
100 g	**lingua salmistrata (brined and braised beef tongue)**
50 g	**cooked ham**
20 g	**black winter truffle**, plus shavings to serve
	salt and ground black pepper

Mix the minced (ground) meat, Parmesan and egg until well combined. Season with salt and pepper and shape the mixture into meatballs slightly larger than a hazelnut. Lightly flour the meatballs, fry them in butter until golden and pat dry with kitchen paper (paper towels). Sauté the mushrooms in oil in a frying pan or skillet, drizzling from time to time with some of the Marsala and making sure that they remain firm and tasty. Cut the cooked mushrooms, tongue, ham and black truffle into strips, then sauté everything in the frying pan for 2 minutes while stirring. Adjust the seasoning with salt and pepper.

FOR THE JUS

300 g	**beef**
250 g	**knuckle bones**
50 ml	**extra-virgin olive oil**
100 g	**white onion**, finely chopped
100 g	**carrot**, finely chopped
100 g	**celery**, finely chopped
25 g	**unsalted butter**, softened
35 g	**plain (all-purpose) flour**
	salt and ground white pepper

Cook a classic Neapolitan ragù with the meat, oil and vegetables. Once cooked, remove any bones and thicken with a white roux.

Preheat the oven to 180°C/350°F. Grease a zuccotto (dome) mould with butter and start to line it with the cooked bucatini, forming a spiral from the bottom. Continue to arrange the bucatini in a spiral until it covers the entire inside surface of the mould. Cover the bucatini lining with a thin layer of chicken forcemeat. Cover the forcemeat with a 1-cm-/½-inch-thick layer of saffron rice to thicken the timbale shell. Setting aside enough bucatini to cover the bottom of the timbale, cut the remaining bucatini into 4–5-cm/1½–2-inch lengths and mix into the filling mixture. Fill the lined case with the filling and finish with a thin layer of forcemeat and a spiral layer of cooked bucatini. Place a tray of water in the oven and bake the timbale mould in the bain-marie for 40 minutes. Then allow to rest for 20 minutes. Turn the timbale out onto a serving dish and glaze with the jus. Finish with a few truffle shavings and the traditional wick in the centre of the shell.

Bejewelled quail

Serves 4

4	**quails**, boned
500 g	**creamy saffron rice filling** (see below)
4 l	**chicken stock**, to cover
40 g	**honey and soy molasses** (see below)
10 g	**caramelized spice mix** (see below)
15 g	**fresh coriander (cilantro)**
5 g	**fresh flowers**
120 g	**spinach and anise cream** (see below)
40 g	**chicken jus**
5 g	**Gremolada** (see page 210)

FOR THE CREAMY SAFFRON RICE FILLING

250 g	**Carnaroli rice**
120 g	**unsalted butter**
1 g	**saffron threads**
½	**stick lemongrass**
60 g	**Parmigiano Reggiano cheese**
60 g	**Comté cheese**
60 g	**dried apricots**, diced
35 g	**raisins or sultanas (golden raisins)**
15 g	**barberries**
25 g	**fresh pork back fat**, cooked
20 g	**veal bone marrow**
10 g	**unblanched almonds**, chopped
3 g	**coriander (cilantro) leaves**, torn
15 g	**red onion**, finely diced
2 g	**chives**, finely chopped
1 g	**coriander (cilantro) stalk**, finely chopped
6 g	**salt**

In a frying pan or skillet, toast the rice in 20 g of the butter, then add the saffron and lemongrass. Moisten with water and cook like a traditional risotto. Then mix the other ingredients into the rice to combine and season with the salt. Allow to cool and set aside.

FOR THE SPINACH AND ANISE CREAM

500 g	**spinach leaves**, washed and trimmed
12 g	**unsalted butter**
12 g	**soft wheat flour** (W index 180–230)
250 g	**chicken stock**
	grated nutmeg and ground star anise, as needed
	salt and ground white pepper

Blanch the spinach for 5 minutes in a large pan of salted water, then refresh in a bowl of iced water. Lightly squeeze the leaves to drain and set aside. In a large pan, make a roux with the butter and flour, then add the stock and thicken by cooking for a few minutes. Add the spinach and blend until smooth and creamy. Season with salt, pepper, nutmeg and star anise.

FOR THE HONEY AND SOY MOLASSES

½	**shallot**, finely diced
10 g	**unsalted butter**
30 g	**soy sauce**
30 g	**glucose syrup**
30 g	**veal stock**

Sauté the shallot in a pan with the butter until soft. Deglaze with the soy sauce, then add the glucose syrup and cook for a few minutes. Incorporate the veal stock and allow to cool.

FOR THE CARAMELIZED SPICE MIX

5 g	**coriander seeds**
4 g	**pink pepper**
1 g	**cumin seeds**
8 g	**caster (superfine) sugar**
0.5 g	**fine sea salt**

Toast all the spices in a pan. In another pan, cook the sugar to a caramel and stop the cooking process by adding the toasted spices and the salt. Coat well in the caramel, transfer to an air-tight container and set aside in a dry place.

ASSEMBLY

Preheat the oven to 70°C/158°F. Lay the boned quails out flat on the work surface and season the belly side with salt. Place a 115–120-g portion of creamy rice in the centre and fold over the sides to cover the filling as much as possible. Wrap the quails tightly in cling film (plastic wrap), place in a pan with enough chicken stock to cover and cook in the oven for 1 hour 20 minutes. Remove the cling film and allow to cool. Immediately before serving, roast the stuffed quails at 210°C/410°F for 9–10 minutes. As soon as they come out of the oven, brush the surface with the honey and soy molasses and sprinkle with the caramelized spice mix. Garnish with torn coriander (cilantro) leaves and flower petals. Slice the quails at the table, serve with the anise-flavoured spinach cream and a tablespoon of chicken jus and top with the gremolada.

Char in a pastry crust

Serves 4

FOR THE CHAR FORCEMEAT

100 g	**trimmings from a large Arctic char**
40 g	**egg white**
	salt and ground white pepper
25 ml	**double (heavy) cream**

Combine the fish trimmings and egg white in a mixing beaker. Season with the salt and ground white pepper. Blend and filter through a fine-mesh sieve (strainer). Transfer the mixture to a chilled bowl placed over a bowl of ice water. Mix in the cream until incorporated and smooth.

FOR THE DUXELLES

500 g	**white mushrooms**
70 g	**shallots**
5 g	**garlic**, minced
25 g	**unsalted butter**
2 g	**thyme leaves**
	salt and ground white pepper

Clean and finely dice the mushrooms. Slice the shallots into julienne strips and sauté in a pan with the garlic and butter for a few minutes. Add the diced mushrooms and cook over a very low heat for 1 hour. Take care that nothing sticks to the pan as all the liquid evaporates without the need to add stock or water. Once a coarse and creamy paste forms, add the thyme leaves. Season with salt and pepper and set aside.

FOR THE CHAR, CHARD AND BLACK TRUFFLE FORCEMEAT

100 g	**swiss chard leaves**, blanched
15 g	**black truffle**, finely chopped
30 g	**black truffle paste**
25 g	**duxelles** (see above)
165 g	**char forcemeat** (see above)

Finely chop the blanched chard and mix with the truffle, the truffle paste and the duxelles into the forcemeat.

FOR THE CRÊPES

400 ml	**fresh milk**
170 g	**soft wheat flour** (W index 180–230)
30 g	**unsalted butter**
15 g	**chopped parsley**
120 g	**egg**
	salt

Mix the ingredients into a batter and cook crêpes that are slightly thicker than usual, as they will be used to wrap the filling before encasing it in puff pastry.

ASSEMBLY

4	**crêpes** (see above)
300 g	**char, chard and black truffle forcemeat** (see above)
260 g	**char fillet steak**
50 g	**mustard**
220 g	**thin puff pastry sheet**
60 g	**egg**
15 ml	**double (heavy) cream**
	Maldon salt

Preheat a convection oven to 200°C/400°F. Lay 2 crêpes on the table with the edges of one side lined up and spread with the forcemeat. Brush the char steak with mustard and position it in the middle of the forcemeat. Wrap the crêpes around the fish, ensuring that it remains in the centre of the forcemeat. Then wrap the parcel in puff pastry, seal the edges and brush with an egg wash made by beating the egg with the cream. Decorate the pastry as desired and bake for 20 minutes. Allow to rest for 5 minutes before serving and slicing at the table.

Panettone alla Milanese

Makes 2 panettoni (1 kg each)

Note: All the ingredients must be at room temperature.

FOR THE FIRST DOUGH

500 g	**soft wheat flour** (W index 320–380)
150 g	**liquid sourdough starter**
250 ml	**water** (at 27°C/81°F)
125 g	**egg yolk**
140 g	**caster (superfine) sugar**
200 g	**unsalted butter**, softened, plus extra for greasing

In a mixer, combine the flour, sourdough starter, water (at 27°C/81°F) and egg yolks and mix for 7 minutes. Add the sugar and knead for 7 minutes. Add the butter and knead for a further 7 minutes until completely incorporated. The dough should be at a temperature of 25–26°C/77–79°F. Transfer to a tall, narrow and butter-greased container and rest at room temperature for 12–15 hours until the dough has tripled in volume.

FOR THE SECOND DOUGH
125 g **soft wheat flour** (W index 180–230)
125 g **egg yolk**
140 g **caster (superfine) sugar**
12 g **acacia honey**
250 g **unsalted butter**, softened
675 g **candied fruit** (50% orange and 50% citron)
12 g **salt**
½ **vanilla pod (bean)**, seeds scraped

The next day, put the risen first dough into the mixer with the flour and knead for 8 minutes. Add the egg yolk and continue to knead for 8 minutes. Add the sugar and honey and knead for a further 8 minutes. Add the butter and knead for a further 12 minutes until all the added ingredients are fully incorporated into the dough.
Drain and dice the candied fruit and add it to the dough with the salt and vanilla seeds. The final temperature of the dough should not exceed 26–27°C/77–79°F. Rest the dough in a tall, narrow and butter-greased container for about 30 minutes. Divide the dough into two 1 kg forms and gather into balls, first folding and stretching to develop structure, and then rotating and compacting. Place the dough balls on a baking tray and rest for about 20 minutes to form a skin. Place the dough balls in individual panettone moulds and prove at 26–27°C/77–79°F until the mould is filled to three-quarters (this should take 5–6 hours).
Preheat the oven to 180°C/350°F and bake for 40–45 minutes until the internal temperature reaches 92°C/198°F. Remove from the oven and hang upside down for 12 hours before unmoulding.

Tiramisù profiteroles

Serves 10

FOR THE CHOUX BUNS (about 50 buns)
50 ml **water**
50 ml **milk**
45 g **unsalted butter**, plus extra for greasing
1,5 g **salt**
1 g **caster (superfine) sugar**
55 g **soft wheat flour** (W index 180–230)
100 g **egg**

Preheat the oven to 180°C/350°F. In a pan, combine the water, milk, butter, salt and sugar and bring to the boil. Add all the flour and stir constantly while cooking until the dough pulls away from the sides of the pan and feels dry when pinched. Transfer to a stand mixer fitted with a paddle attachment and run the mixer. As soon as the dough cools a little, start adding the egg, a little at a time, until the dough is smooth and thick. Using a piping (pastry) bag, pipe choux buns on a perforated baking tray greased with butter. Bake for 20–25 minutes with the vent open.

FOR THE PASTRY CREAM
175 g **egg yolk**
110 g **caster (superfine) sugar**
vanilla seeds, as needed
10 g **rice starch**
20 g **cornflour (cornstarch)**
125 ml **double (heavy) cream**
220 ml **fresh milk**
½ **vanilla pod (bean)**

Using a whisk, beat the egg yolk with the sugar, followed in succession by the scraped vanilla seeds, rice starch and cornflour (cornstarch). In a pan, combine the cream with the milk and vanilla pod (bean) and bring to the boil. Add to the egg mixture and carefully stir to incorporate. Transfer the mixture into a pan and cook to 82°C/180°F while stirring briskly. Quickly cool in a blast chiller and set aside in the fridge.

FOR THE HAZELNUT AND COFFEE PRALINE
125 g **caster (superfine) sugar**
125 g **hazelnuts**
sunflower oil, as needed
100 g **coffee paste**
salt

In a pan, cook the sugar to a caramel. Pour the caramel onto a baking tray lined with a Silpat. Allow to cool completely to room temperature.
Meanwhile, roast the hazelnuts at 160°C/325°F for about 20 minutes. Allow to cool completely to room temperature. Blend the caramel with the hazelnuts, adding sunflower oil as desired until very smooth, then add the coffee paste and season with salt.

FOR THE COFFEE CREAM
500 g **pastry cream** (see above)
300 g **hazelnut and coffee praline**
100 ml **soft-whipped cream**

Mix the pastry cream with the praline, then incorporate the soft-whipped cream.

FOR THE MASCARPONE CREAM
500 g **mascarpone cheese**
200 ml **double (heavy) cream**
1 g **salt**
1 **vanilla pod (bean)**, split in half lengthways and seeds scraped out
40 ml **water**
150 g **caster (superfine) sugar**
125 g **egg yolk**
30 g **isinglass** (rehydrated in 150 g cold water)

Mix the mascarpone with the cream, salt and vanilla seeds. Make a pâte à bombe by cooking the 40 ml water and the sugar to 121°C/250°F to make a syrup. In a mixer, whisk the egg yolk and add the syrup in a thin stream. Then add the isinglass, previously soaked in the 150 g cold water. Allow the mixture to cool to 25–30°C/77–86°F before adding the mascarpone mixture. Continue to whisk for a few minutes until the cream is fluffy and stable.

ASSEMBLY
30 g **cocoa powder**
5g **instant coffee**

Carefully fill the choux buns with plenty of pastry cream. Dip them into the mascarpone cream and tap with a fork to remove the excess. Assemble the profiteroles into a pyramid and finish by dusting with 30 g cocoa powder and 5 g instant coffee.

THE WINE CELLAR (CANTINA)

Located on the lowest floor, below the Galleria's most trodden passageway, the Wine Cellar is set in one of the city's most fascinating subterranean areas. It has a stone floor, fir-wood window frames and skylights of glass and brass – the same as in the Galleria – as well as blood-red painted walls.

Initially conceived as a simple place for sommeliers and waiters to quickly select the wine chosen by the restaurant's customers, the space proved so hospitable that it eventually became an integral part of the restaurant. Tables of fine French craftsmanship were therefore eventually added in the centre of the room. The Wine Cellar is primarily a tasting and sales space for our two thousand or so varieties of wine, selected with great depth of producers and vintages from Italy, France and the rest of the world. But this is also a dining space, often wine-themed, which can accommodate up to fourteen diners. The Wine Cellar's menu features recipes inspired by classic Milanese gastronomy, including cakes that conjure up a real sense of occasion.

ÉZEAUX
GRANDS ÉCHÉZEAUX
ANNÉE 2003

GAJA
KRUG

BLACK BREAD

From breakfast to dinner, the baking of bread is more than just a formality: we strive to produce leavened loaves with real personality and originality, in the true Italian tradition. In our view, one of the most successful and suitable breads to accompany the tastings in the cellar – the wines, cheeses, cured meats – is 'pane nero', a sourdough bread with flax and barley seeds. Dark and almost malty, it has a very rich flavour and great versatility.

2005
MISE EN BOUTEILLES
Meursaul
APPELLATION MEURSAULT CONTRÔLÉE

RICHEBOURG
APPELLATION RICHEBOURG CONTROLÉE
11.323 Bouteilles Récoltées
LES ASSOCIÉS-GÉRANTS
BOUTEILLE Nº 03125
ANNÉE 2010
Mise en bouteille au domaine

Gorgonzola dolce, mascarpone and walnut cake

GORGONZOLA DOLCE, MASCARPONE AND WALNUT CAKE

How many times, as kids, did we drool over those sweet gorgonzola, mascarpone and walnut cakes that we could see beckoning to us, under the opulence of a veil of its glaze, from the windows of the city's best delicatessens? Many times! So much so that we decided to serve these cakes in our restaurants, too, especially at Christmas, or on other special occasions.
Studying traditional Lombardy-Piedmontese recipe books from the nineteenth century, we discovered that, as is often the case, the fortuitous pairing of gorgonzola and mascarpone was actually the result of rustic shrewdness: the master cheesemakers didn't want to throw away leftover gorgonzola dolce, even if it was perhaps imperfect or a little past its prime, so they added leftover mascarpone to it. This combination of two cheeses was flattened inside domed zuccotto-like moulds, inverted and then embellished with walnut kernels. This recipe not only ensured that precious ingredients were not wasted, but also created a dish with a sumptuous richness of flavour and creaminess that makes us close our eyes from sheer pleasure.

BRIE, MASCARPONE AND SMOKED SALMON CAKE

It is difficult to identify the precise historical origins of this dish. There are certainly initial traces of it at the nineteenth-century French royal court, but later it appears in those fascinating counter-service delicatessens that began to pop up in big cities, from Paris to Lyon. This idea of premises overflowing with good things is a model that we have eagerly adopted, protecting us from the suffocating rise of large retailers. Originally, a horizontal cut was made in the top of the cake, which was then filled with thin slices of smoked salmon. We changed the arrangement of the brie, alternating it with thin layers of mascarpone, mixed with cognac and dill. We repeat the layering at least twice and then top it with more slivers of salmon. Then, we slice it at the table, like a real cake.
This dish hints at our most important festivities, particularly Christmas, and that is why we love to serve it in the scenic setting of our Cellar, pairing it with wines that can match its quality. This is a cake that is a little more complicated than it may seem. But the degree of ultimate satisfaction it provides is a veritable blast from the past.

GRANDS ÉCHÉZEAUX
ANNÉE 2003
Mise en bouteille au domaine

Brie, mascarpone and smoked salmon cake

The Wine cellar (or Cantina) was not included in Cracco's original architectural plans for the Galleria. The chance discovery of a potentially interesting space under the Gallery's busiest thoroughfare gave rise to a wine table that basks in its own distinctive glow, while simultaneously crying out to be shared by all.

In addition to cured meats and cheeses, the Wine cellar's menu includes two stand-out pies: one stuffed with sweet gorgonzola, mascarpone and walnuts, and the other full of brie, more mascarpone and smoked salmon. Once again, we are overwhelmed by the busy, tasty recipes, creating a truly festive air.

SASSICAIA
SOLAIA
CASTELLO DI AMA

RECIPES
FROM THE CANTINA

Black bread

Makes 4 loaves (900 g each)

80 g	**linseeds**
240 g	**water** (at room temperature)
400 g	**liquid sourdough starter** (at 4°/39°F)
200 g	**soft wheat flour** (W index 180–230) **mixed with millet, linseed, sesame seeds and sunflower seeds**
600 g	**remilled durum wheat semolina**
200 g	**einkorn flour**
1 kg	**medium-strong white flour** (W index 240–300), plus extra for dusting
20 g	**caster (superfine) sugar**
40 g	**orzo (soluble barley)**
1 g	**dried yeast**
1.2 l	**water** (at 4°/39°F)
50 g	**salt**

Roast the linseeds at 165°C/329°F for 15 minutes. Add the hot seeds to the 240 g room-temperature water and stir to form a gel. Allow to cool before use. In a mixer, combine the sourdough starter, wheat flour and seed mixture, semolina, einkorn flour, white flour, sugar, orzo, yeast and the 1.2 litres water (at 4°C/39°F). Mix for 5 minutes to form a dough, then rest for 40 minutes. Knead the dough, adding the toasted seeds and salt one-third at a time, for about 20 minutes. The final temperature of the dough should be 26–27°C/79–81°F. Stretch and fold the dough to develop its structure, gathering it into a ball by rotating and compacting. Repeat the operation four times every 40 minutes. Then divide the dough into 1-kg portions and gather into balls by rotating and compacting. Place each one on a baking tray lightly dusted with flour and rest for 20 minutes to allow a skin to form.
Turn the dough balls upside down, leaving the skin side in contact with the work surface, then press lightly and shape the sides into a square. Fold the dough in thirds like a letter and gently roll up to form loaves. Place the dough into four loaf tins dusted with flour. Prove at room temperature: for 4 hours if baking on the same the day, or for 2 hours at room temperature and then for 16 hours in the fridge if baking the next day. Bake in a static (non-convection) oven at 250°C/482°F top heat and 235°C/455°F bottom heat for about 40 minutes.

Gorgonzola dolce, mascarpone and walnut cake

Serves 8

500 g	**Gorgonzola dolce cheese**
300 g	**fresh mascarpone cheese**
150 g	**chives**
	ground white pepper
150 g	**chopped shelled walnuts**
	walnuts, to decorate
	Black bread to serve (see left)

Line the sides of a 24-cm-/9½-inch-diameter round cake tin with an acetate strip. Remove the rind from the gorgonzola and use a soft-cheese slicer to cut slices of just over 1 cm/½ inch in thickness. Arrange the slices over the bottom of the cake tin, then cover them with a layer of mascarpone mixed with 10 g of finely chopped chives and a sprinkling of freshly ground white pepper. Sprinkle the mascarpone with chopped walnuts and then repeat the sequence with another gorgonzola layer. Finish with a mascarpone layer and level the surface with a spatula. Decorate with whole walnut kernels. Refrigerate for 3–4 hours to set. Serve sliced like a real cake, accompanied by toasted Black bread.

Brie, mascarpone and smoked salmon cake

Serves 8

500 g	**brie**
10 g	**finely chopped dill**
150 g	**fresh mascarpone cheese**
100 g	**unsalted butter, softened**
10 g	**Cognac**
200 g	**smoked salmon**
	ground white pepper

Cut thin slices of brie and line the base of a 20-cm-/8-inch-diameter cake tin. Mix the dill and a pinch of white pepper into the mascarpone. Mix the butter with the cognac until combined. Spread a thin layer of mascarpone mixture over the brie, then cover the top of the mascarpone with thin slices of smoked salmon. Cover the salmon with a very thin layer of the butter mixture. Make another layer of brie and one of mascarpone, then cover the whole cake with smoked salmon, including the sides. Refrigerate for 3 hours (optionally, you can cover the cake with aspic as this ensures that the cake keeps better and the moisture of the salmon is retained).

ROMANÉE-ST-VIVANT
APPELLATION ROMANÉE-ST-VIVANT CONTROLÉE
ANNÉE 2015
GRANDS ÉCHÉZEAUX
APPELLATION GRANDS ÉCHÉZEAUX CONTROLÉE
ANNÉE 2003
Meursault

CHEESE

In our first restaurant, the trolley contained only Italian cheeses, made by painstaking artisans who have always produced small, precious varieties of cheese. These were classic pure flavours, not too complex, processed or flavoured with other ingredients.
Since we've been in the Galleria, we've decided to extend our range to cheeses from other countries, such as Switzerland, France and even the United States, because nobody wants their cuisine to be too constrained by patriotism!
In the pantry, we keep about twenty cheeses, including cow, goat and sheep varieties. They are all variations of the historic Bitto, Pecorino di Fossa, Taleggio, gorgonzola and Parmigiano Reggiano. We also have a blue cheese produced in the United States by an Italian gentleman who succeeded in adapting the Roquefort recipe to the local cows' milk: it's fabulous!

INDEX OF RECIPES

GLOSSARY

APPLIANCE
A preparation composed of multiple ingredients, intended to create part of a recipe (for example: 'crêpe maker,' 'quiche maker,' etc.). A synonym for appliance is "compound."

BISQUE
A typical preparation of French cuisine, this fish stock—most often shellfish—can serve as a preparation or ingredient in compound preparations.

CEVICHE
A technique of marinating raw fish with lemon juice, coriander and chilli pepper. It is widely used in South American cuisine, particularly in Peru.

CONFIT
A technique of prolonged, low-temperature cooking in oil or fat, originally used to preserve food. Confit tomatoes, dried in the oven and preserved in flavoured oil, are quite common.

WHITE MIX
A mixture generally composed of chocolate and cocoa butter, sprayed using a special compressor to create a velvety effect on cakes, single-serving cuisines or miniature pastries.

PACOJET
A machine for the express churning of ice cream, used primarily in the catering industry.

KNEADING
The process of kneading a portion of leavened dough by hand to give it strength and structure, creating a smooth, well-filled bubble.

SALAMANDER
A radiant-heat grill, widely used in professional kitchens, that allows for browning ingredients and preparations.

SEARING
A technique that involves searing meat or fish to create an external surface that locks in the juices during cooking, thus producing more tender, richer, and more succulent meat.

SILPAT
A non-stick silicone mat used for lining baking trays in cooking and pastry-making in place of parchment paper or grease.

PUFFING
A technique that involves frying and puffing dry foods by immersion in boiling oil for brief moments and at high temperatures.

W INDEX
An indicator of the strength of the flour, meaning its ability to develop a gluten network.

AKNOWLEDGEMENTS

This book is a long-held dream, the diary of a journey that began among shared desires, visions and obstinacies. It is the landing of different souls setting out toward a destination that, in the end, summarizes the trajectories of each one. It is a collective wave rising with the contribution of each and every one. It is a place where time has ceased to be a straight line, a whole that has brought knowledge and fragility, intuitions and silences, the generosity of those who offer the best of themselves without fear of losing anything. Exchanges, confluences, heartbeats that have learned to proceed in unison. Invisible hands guided by a single vision, a reason that drives us to profound and sincere thanks.

Thanks to Pierpaolo, Maurizio, Alberto, Sebastiano and the enchanted world of TOILETPAPER, which we have always observed with wonder, loving annoyance and attraction. Thank you for inspiring us and making us believe that the unusual can take the forms of irony and beauty—after all, we all need a little TOILETPAPER.

Thanks to Phaidon and L'Ippocampo, who have trusted us when we were still a shapeless mass. They welcomed us without fear, following our rhythm even when it was uncertain, when the path was still lost among the curves.

Thanks to Gabriele, who courageously responded to a voiceless call, transforming visions into words, weaving distant worlds into a single narrative.

Thanks to all our brigade, who faced every request, even the craziest, with grit and heart, patience and dedication, seriousness and passion. Every day they build a world that then also becomes a little yours.

Finally, thanks to you, dear reader, who, by some strange coincidence, has chosen to venture into this world.

Carlo Cracco and Luca Sacchi

Since this work is driven by creative liberty, I'd like to take one too. Thank you to Carlo because he knows how to lead without imposing, walk with us without ever distancing us, stop when we need to let go.

He taught us that every fruit has its time and that waiting is an act of passion: it's thanks to him that this dream has taken shape in the most mature season. Thank you because your every word and every gesture leaves a mark that never fades.

Luca Sacchi

Concept and Images by TOILETPAPER

Photo: Pierpaolo Ferrari, Alberto Zanetti, Maurizio Cattelan
Art directed by: Sebastiano Mastroeni

Colour and digital development: Anna Tallone
Digital operator: Tommaso Bressan at Studio Santaveronica
Production: Stefania Biliato
Thanks to: Lorenzo Zavatta, Chiara Quadri, Juliano Araujo, Niko Dekovic, Fabio Bordessa, Jacopo Todorov, Andrea Ceppi, Elisa Zaccanti, Bianca Luini, Benedetta Maiani, Lisa Colombo, Cecilia Salerni, Jenny Jia, Alessandro Pagani, Laura Moroni, Andrea Ghisalberti

Phaidon Press Limited
2 Cooperage Yard
London E15 2QR

Phaidon Press Inc.
111 Broadway
New York, NY 10006

Phaidon SARL
55, rue Traversière
75012 Paris

phaidon.com

First published 2025

ISBN 978 1 83729 015 4

A CIP catalogue record for this book is available from the British Library and the Library of Congress.

Commissioning Editor: Emilia Terragni
Production Controller: Gary Hayes

Printed in Italy

Butter should always be unsalted, unless otherwise specified. All spices are freshly ground, unless otherwise specified. Eggs and individual vegetables and fruits, such as carrots and apples, are assumed to be medium, unless otherwise specified. All sugar is white caster (superfine) sugar and all brown sugar is cane or demerara unless otherwise specified. All cream is 36–40% fat heavy whipping cream unless otherwise specified. All milk is full-fat (whole) at 3% fat, homogenized and lightly pasteurized, unless otherwise specified. All yeast is fresh, unless otherwise specified. All salt is fine sea salt, unless otherwise specified. Cooking times are for guidance only, as individual ovens vary. If using a conventional oven, follow the manufacturer's instructions concerning oven temperatures. Exercise a high level of caution when following recipes involving any potentially hazardous activity, including the use of high temperatures, open flames and when deep-frying. In particular, when deep-frying, add food carefully to avoid splashing, wear long sleeves, and never leave the pan unattended. Some recipes include raw or very lightly cooked eggs, meat, or fish, and fermented products. These should be avoided by the elderly, infants, pregnant women, convalescents, and anyone with an impaired immune system. Exercise caution when making fermented products, ensuring all equipment is spotlessly clean, and seek expert advice if in any doubt. When no quantity is specified, for example of oils, and sugars used for finishing dishes or for deep frying, quantities are discretionary and flexible. All herbs, shoots, flowers and leaves should be picked fresh from a clean source. Do exercise caution when foraging for ingredients, which should only be eaten if an expert has deemed them safe to eat. In particular, do not gather wild mushrooms yourself before seeking the advice of an expert who has confirmed their suitability for human consumption. As some species of mushrooms have been known to cause allergic reaction and illness, do take extra care when cooking and eating mushrooms and do seek immediate medical help if you experience a reaction after preparing or eating them.